LOOKS

LOOKS
A PHILOSOPHICAL DIALOGUE

Nicholas J. Pappas

Algora Publishing
New York

Library of Congress Cataloging-in-Publication Data

Names: Pappas, Nicholas J., author.
Title: Looks : a philosophical dialogue / Nicholas J. Pappas.
Description: New York : Algora Publishing, [2022] | Summary: "Life works
    best when people value us for more than our looks. In these pages, Model
    and a philosopher friend reflect on the subtleties of life, revealing
    insights and finding ways to develop deeper, more meaningful ties with
    our own inner self and the other people in our lives"   Provided by
    publisher.
Identifiers: LCCN 2022053224 (print) | LCCN 2022053225 (ebook) | ISBN
    9781628945034 (trade paperback) | ISBN 9781628945041 (hardcover) | ISBN
    9781628945058 (pdf)
Subjects: LCSH: Aesthetics   Philosophical aspects.
Classification: LCC BH39 .P245 2022 (print) | LCC BH39 (ebook) | DDC
    111/.85   dc23/eng/20230130
LC record available at https://lccn.loc.gov/2022053224
LC ebook record available at https://lccn.loc.gov/2022053225

Printed in the United States

More Books by Nick Pappas
from Algora Publishing

Controvert, or On the Lie and Other Philosophical Dialogues, 2008

Aristocrat, and The Community: Two Philosophical Dialogues, 2010

On Awareness: A Collection of Philosophical Dialogues, 2011

Belief and Integrity: Philosophical Dialogues, 2011

On Strength, 2012

On Freedom: A Philosophical Dialogue, 2014

On Life: Philosophical Dialogues, 2015

On Love: A Philosophical Dialogue, 2016

On Destiny: A Philosophical Dialogue, 2016

On Wisdom: A Philosophical Dialogue, 2017

All of Health: A Philosophical Dialogue, 2018

On Education: A Philosophical Dialogue, 2018

On Power: A Philosophical Dialogue, 2019

On Ideas: A Philosophical Dialogue, 2020

On Passivity: A Philosophical Dialogue, 2021

On Authority: A Philosophical Dialogue, 2021

On Violence: A Philosophical Dialogue, 2022

INTRODUCTION

Appearances, looks, how do we get beyond them? They are our constant companions throughout life. It goes to extremes. When we know someone of advanced years whose appearance is poor, at best, we are sometimes shocked to discover an old photo of them in their youth, their prime. They were beautiful. And this realization, this awareness of what they were, it changes our evaluation of them.

Yes, you will say, but I am not that shallow. I see the inner beauty, the soul. While it's nice to see an old one in their prime, it doesn't change my opinion of them.

Well, I'll tell you, not too many people are as deep as you are, my friend. Why else do the good looking fear losing their looks? They, and we, are shallow. We know the advantage looks bring. We know not so many people are deep, not so many peer into the depths of the soul. We even believe, consciously or not, that the soul takes its shape from the exterior. So firm is the belief in looks that those with them fret themselves awake at night. What dreadful things will happen once they lose their looks? What we see in the mirror is what we are.

Point taken. But we need mirrors held up to the soul.

Tell that to someone who lives by their looks. What does it mean to live by your looks? It's a desperate sort of life, if you ask me. But isn't all life desperate? You're never quite certain where you stand. One minute you're the best looking person in the room; the next minute someone stunning walks in; you have to reevaluate where you stand.

Inner beauty never has to reevaluate that way.

I think, old friend, that it does. I know this is heresy, but there it is. Some are more beautiful on the inside than others, and people know it. Which is the more bitter pill to swallow? Someone is better looking than I am, or someone is... better.

Yes, but what people know about the inner realm is limited, to say the least. I don't think people compete on the inside the way they do on the outside. How can they? They don't know much about what's within when all they care about is on the surface.

You make it sound like there aren't inner looks, appearances. People do have inner mirrors; they do study them; and they have more ability to 'make up' their inner self than they do on the outside. On the outside we can wear flattering clothing, and so on. But it only does so much. On the inside, the sky is the limit. We can pretend to be whatever we like. And if we practice it long enough we actually become whatever we like. Exterior looks are more honest; there's less space for trickery.

You exaggerate. There isn't that much flexibility on the inside. Who hasn't wished at one time or other to be, for instance, more patient? Can we pretend, successfully, to be more patient? No. It is extremely hard to change the interior. It's much easier to change the outside through diet or exercise. Beyond that, we can even have plastic surgery to appear the way we wish. There is no such surgery in the heart, mind, or soul.

I'd like to hear what a philosopher has to say about this.

So would I. I'd love to hear him talk to a very beautiful man, someone who has experienced all there is in the world that comes of good looks.

What if the philosopher hasn't experienced these things?

Sometimes the clearer view comes from those not directly involved.

The clearer view, perhaps. But what about insight? You can't have insights unless you've been there. You have to know it from the inside out. There is no other way to see all there is to see. You can have a clear view of a house from a distance, but you don't know what goes on within unless you're inside.

True enough. But each of us has insights into the world. They can't be had without being us.

Yes, but nearly everyone believes in looks, those who have them and those who don't. We want to experience what the beautiful experience. And if it's true that the grass is always greener on the other side, we want that lawn.

I don't. I'm content with the average looking man I am. But, that said, I do confess I wonder. I want to know what the beautiful know. I want to experience what they experience, if only once.

What do you expect they experience?

I don't know. It's a sort of power, I suppose. A power they don't have to will. A power just given to them.

Sure, but isn't it like a diamond in the rough? It needs to be cut, made to sparkle. Who can do that cutting?

Who can do that cutting in anyone?

Yes, but the pressure is on when it comes to beautiful people. Much more is at stake.

What, in terms of human beauty? Don't you think we have to cut the internal diamonds as well?

I do. But everyone doesn't witness this internal business. You and I can make changes that very few see. Not so when all eyes are on you. The audience is aware of every move you make. Every change is scrutinized no end.

The beautiful need some sort of darkness to protect them as they change.

A philosopher can provide such cover.

How?

Through subtle adjustments, things not everyone will notice.

The philosopher is patient; he has a longer range plan.

Yes, though sometimes he must compel the beautiful to rive the knot.

How does the soul of the beautiful grow knotted?

Through unsuccessful resistance to the prying eyes of the crowd.

Why resist? What's wrong with being adored?

I wouldn't know. Would you?

We're alike, average in looks. When we walk into a room people don't light up. Attention doesn't center on us. We inspire no one at first glance.

And we're not on the run. We have our privacy, our containment within ourselves. No one is trying to pry their way in, to see what there is to see inside.

We're hoping our philosopher can show us inside the beautiful. Are we as bad as those who pry?

A philosopher doesn't meddle. A philosopher must be invited in. Above all else, his conversation must be friendly, not pressured or forced. And through this kind of talk we have our best chance to see.

Then let's see what we can see.

—Nick Pappas

Looks, A Philosophical Dialogue

Characters:
    Director
    Model

Scene:
    Island resort

~ Again

Model: I just can't believe I ran into you here, Director! How long has it been?

Director: Years.

Model: Too many years. I can't believe my luck. It's so good to see you.

Director: It's good to see you, Model. How have you been?

Model: Honestly? Just okay.

Director: Sometimes okay is good.

Model: By 'just okay' I mean not so good.

Director: What's wrong? Is your career going badly?

Model: No, my career is going very well.

Director: Is it your love life?

Model: It's... everything.

Director: I'm sorry to hear it. Do you remember when we used to talk about everything?

Model: I do. You always said to take everything one thing at a time until you've worked it all through.

Director: And sometimes you have to go over each thing again and again.

Model: I remember. We used to really talk, didn't we?

Director: We really did. So let's start with love. How are things there?

Model: Miserable.

Director: Why?

Model: Because I'll never have love.

Director: I don't understand. Why not?

Model: Because no one loves me for what I am.

Director: What are you?

Model: Well, we seem to have gotten very deep in very little time. What are you, Director?

Director: I'm a philosopher. What are you?

Model: Little better than a mannequin.

Director: Aren't you being a little too hard on yourself?

Model: Am I? I mean, what do I do? I wear clothes and people take pictures of me.

Director: And no one loves you for this?

Model: No, people do love me for this.

Director: Then why will you never have love? Or don't you love the people who love you for this?

Model: I don't.

Director: What sort of people do you love?

Model: People who distinguish themselves.

Director: I take it that doesn't include those who are distinguished by their looks.

Model: It certainly doesn't. I'm looking for something other than looks.

Director: Something like artistic ability?

Model: I do love artists.

Director: And none of them love you back?

Model: They love me for my looks.

Director: Then why do you love them?

Model: Because they have talent.

Director: But you love them and they love you. That sounds good. But you're telling me something else.

Model: I am. I wish there were more... to me.

~ BRAINS

Director: Well, you live in just the right historical time.

Model: What do you mean?

Director: We might be on the cusp of genetically engineering people to have beautiful looks.

Model: You know, I've thought about that. But tell me why you think the time is right for me.

Director: If everyone can be 'beautiful', some will look for beauty in other things.

Model: I've thought that very thought! I want to have those other things. What do you think they are?

Director: They'll have to do with the brain.

Model: Yes, but I have a worry here.

Director: What worry?

Model: We'll engineer and manufacture powerful brains.

Director: Ah, but there's something you don't know.

Model: Tell me what.

Director: Power isn't the thing.

Model: You, who have such a powerful brain, can say that. But I don't believe it.

Director: You need a certain amount of power, sure. But don't you know? Think of computers.

Model: The brain is too often compared to computers. It's not the same sort of thing.

Director: I agree. But hear me out on just this one comparison. Suppose you have a computer running at speed ten.

Model: Speed ten?

Director: Suppose that means it's very fast.

Model: Okay.

Director: And suppose this computer at speed ten is bogged down with many inefficient programs and processes.

Model: It won't be very fast.

Director: No. And what's worse, it's cluttered with junk of every sort. Now imagine we have a computer at speed one.

Model: One means slow?

Director: Yes. But suppose it's lean and mean. It runs only optimized code and does one or a handful of things very, very well. Which would you rather have?

Model: I'd rather have the clean computer at speed one.

Director: So much for the power of the human brain.

Model: Okay, but obviously the ideal is to have a lean and mean brain running at speed ten.

Director: But the faster the brain the more the risk.

Model: How so?

Director: If you're a ten and everyone else is, on average, a five or a six, might you not come to think you always know best?

Model: Sure.

Director: Can you learn what's best if you always think you know best?

Model: No, you can't.

Director: What effect will that have?

Model: You'll likely be inefficient.

Director: You'll squander the power of your brain.

Model: Yes. But in the future all brains might be clocked at ten. No one will be smarter than anyone else. The problem of thinking you know best goes away.

Director: Maybe it does. But I think the scenario you describe is either a dream or a nightmare. I'm not sure which.

Model: Why a nightmare?

Director: I find it hard to say.

Model: Oh, come on. I can imagine how it might be a nightmare. But why a dream?

Director: Equality might facilitate harmonious communication.

Model: But not if certain people clutter their minds.

Director: So order becomes the sought-after trait.

Model: Order? Really?

Director: Let me shift things a bit. Cleanliness becomes the sought-after trait.

Model: Cleanliness isn't quite the opposite of clutter. But clutter can make a mess. And messes can grow filthy. So I like the idea of cleanliness. I like it very much.

Director: Then you'll like what I have to say.

Model: Tell me.

Director: Cleanliness, today, to some—*is* the most desired trait.

~ CLEAN

Model: I want to know those people!

Director: You know one already. Me.

Model: Do you think my mind is... dirty?

Director: I think it could use some cleaning up.

Model: What tells you this is the case?

Director: The fact that you're not happy.

Model: The clean are happy?

Director: Happier than the soiled.

Model: You really don't need to be anything other than clean?

Director: Well, you could stand to be a little... mean.

Model: Ha! Mean? What do you mean? You're one to speak. You're more gentle than mean. Would you ever give gentleness up?

Director: Trade it in for happiness? I don't know.

Model: Maybe there's a way to have both.

Director: If you can tell me how, you'll distinguish yourself apart from your looks.

Model: Then I really want to tell you how.

Director: So tell.

Model: It's so simple I can't believe you haven't thought of it already! All you have to do is speak cruel words, gently.

Director: Is this something you do?

Model: I have a hard time being mean.

Director: When is it best to be mean?

Model: When dealing with the unkind.

Director: We give them what they deserve?

Model: Yes.

Director: Do you know what you deserve?

Model: I don't.

Director: I'll tell you. You deserve praise for distinguished thought.

Model: You're just teasing me.

Director: No, I'm really not. Not many think to combine gentle and cruel.

Model: Is that what it takes? Unusual combinations?

Director: Unusual combinations can open the way for further thought.

Model: I'd like to be known as an opener of ways.

Director: Open ways help keep our minds clean.

Model: I'd like to try to open another way.

Director: How about combining clean with something unusual?

Model: Alright. Clean minds need the power of dirt.

Director: I have no idea where you're going with this.

Model: Dirt can be grit, right? And grit is abrasive. It can be used for scrubbing.

Director: Well, grit is usually particles of stone or sand.

Model: Okay. Let me try again. Clean minds need contrast.

Director: Can you say more?

Model: They need to know the unclean, in order to know they're clean.

Director: And if everyone is clean?

Model: We can't really know what clean means. It's sort of like if everyone is beautiful. We can't really know what beauty is. There's no defining contrast here.

Director: But with beauty we said we'd look for other distinguishing features. What distinguishing features would clean minds seek?

Model: I'm not sure.

~ DIRT

Director: Maybe you had it right.

Model: What do you mean?

Director: Maybe these minds would look for dirt.

Model: Okay. But what does 'dirt' stand for here?

Director: Haven't you heard people say, 'I've got the dirt on him?'

Model: Of course.

Director: Well, what if 'dirt' just means little-known information?

Model: But 'dirt' suggests it's negative information.

Director: Maybe that's just a prejudice.

Model: How so?

Director: We need dirt. Dirt makes things grow.

Model: That's true.

Director: So to say, 'I've got the dirt on him,' means to say you know what makes him grow.

Model: And growth is good.

Director: Yes, when it means to flourish.

Model: But what does a clean mind do with this dirt? And how is it any different than what a not-so-clean mind would do?

Director: The clean mind learns from the other's dirt, then gets some dirt of its own and spreads it around.

Model: It makes itself unclean?

Director: Yes. Unclean and ready for growth.

Model: Ha! I like that very much. And I must be ready to grow, since you said I could use some cleaning up!

Director: Yes. But what if someone tells us the dirt is actually clean?

Model: No, dirt is dirty, no two ways about it.

Director: Well, as we agree, you have some dirt to work with. But maybe you need more.

Model: Where should I find it?

Director: Why not start by looking for the dirt of the artists you know?

Model: Are you suggesting I might take some of their dirt and spread it around in my soul?

Director: Ah, the soul. Yes, take that dirt and spread it around. Then plant some seeds.

Model: Where will I find the seeds?

Director: Look for growths you admire, then collect their seeds.

Model: It sounds so simple. But I'm going call my dirt something else. I'm going to call it earth.

Director: I think you should. Earth is a wonderful thing.

~ SIMPLE

Model: It's so strange.

Director: What is?

Model: In an age of bioengineering, earth takes us back to a much simpler time.

Director: I'm not one who believes times were ever simpler.

Model: Why not? Look at how complex the world is today!

Director: The world has always been complex.

Model: How can you say that?

Director: Because of philosophy.

Model: What does philosophy show?

Director: Tell me, would you say the Middle Ages were relatively simple?

Model: Yes, of course. Many people look to that as a better time.

Director: There was philosophy in the Middle Ages. It was very complex.

Model: Maybe it needed to be complex because times were so simple. What? What's wrong?

Director: You almost silenced me.

Model: What do you mean?

Director: That was a profound observation.

Model: Thank you.

Director: But I don't think it's true.

Model: Of course you don't. Why wouldn't it be true?

Director: Because sophisticated philosophical writings presuppose a sophisticated audience.

Model: What does your philosophy presuppose?

Director: You know I don't write much.

Model: What does that say about your audience?

Director: They haven't got much time to read. But you're part of my audience, Model. You and people like you.

Model: You don't want a broader audience than that?

Director: There have been times when philosophy has achieved great audiences. That's not what I think it needs now.

Model: Why not?

Director: It's too exposed.

Model: What do you mean?

Director: Certain growths need less exposure in order to thrive. Philosophy is one.

Model: Okay, but we live in an age when anything said can spread throughout the entire Earth in the blink of an eye.

Director: That's what I'm getting at, my friend. Philosophy doesn't want the whole world gawking at it today.

Model: It only wants part of the world to see?

Director: Yes, its friends.

Model: How can it ensure it's only friends?

Director: By writing in a certain way.

Model: So philosophy must be obscure.

Director: No. Philosophy must simple—and boring.

Model: Ha! I don't believe you there. I thrilled at some of the things you wrote.

Director: That's because they were written for you and your kind.

Model: My kind?

Director: Your kindred. The rest, they see nothing exciting here.

Model: That's quite an art—exciting to some, boring to the rest.

Director: Yes, it is. The writer must walk a fine line.

Model: I wish I could share my physical beauty only with friends.

Director: Get out of the business you're in.

Model: I have enough money now that I could.

Director: What stops you?

Model: Nothing.

- Flavor, Nothing, Further

Model: Can you imagine if the whole world grew bored of looks?

Director: Why would it?

Model: Have you ever had a genetically modified strawberry?

Director: I have.

Model: They look perfect, don't they?

Director: They do.

Model: But how do they taste?

Director: Not as good as the wild strawberries I knew as a youth.

Model: Exactly! That's why the whole world might grow bored of engineered looks. They lack flavor.

Director: And the world would come to long for natural looks?

Model: Yes, and all their mutations.

Director: But what if we just keep on engineering away, making 'better' and 'better' looks?

Model: More expensive looks, you mean.

Director: Of course. The best looks would cost the most. That's the real news here. Money and looks would be combined.

Model: Oh, what's new about that? Looks and money have bred since time began.

Director: But that sort of breeding is uncertain. Engineering isn't. That's a big change.

Model: Beauty on demand. Give me a good mutation any day.

Director: Would you say that when it comes to more than looks?

Model: You're talking about the brain?

Director: The brain will be engineered, too. We'll have the same problems here. Is the most expensive brain the most beautiful? Or is it the brain with the most striking mutations?

Model: Maybe it's the brain that can focus on the nothing.

Director: The nothing?

Model: Oh, you know. The nothing as described in certain religions and philosophies.

Director: Any brain can do that.

Model: But how many do? Nothing is its own sort of beauty.

Director: If you've been thinking that, I—

Model: But isn't it true? Nothing is the ultimate alternative!

Director: That doesn't make it good.

Model: But even if not good, at least it's unique.

Director: I don't know about that. I think 'nothing' is more common than you think.

Model: Then how can I be unique, other than for my looks?

Director: By taking what you've been given, and taking it further than we thought possible. That's what makes anyone unique.

Model: Where can I take my looks?

Director: I was talking about your brains.

Model: How do I take them further?

Director: You can't be unique unless you figure that out on your own.

Model: But you can help. Can't you?

Director: I can give you ideas. But you have to make sense of them yourself.

Model: So give me an idea.

Director: Here's one to start with. Looks are more important than brains.

~ Disgust, What You Do

Model: For many I think that's true. Some value brains; more value looks. And that's why I'm disgusted with myself.

Director: You're disgusted with yourself because others are wrong?

Model: I'm disgusted because I make a living from their mistake!

Director: Then set them straight.

Model: How?

Director: End your modeling career.

Model: And do what? Take up professional chess?

Director: Get a regular sort of job.

Model: They'll put me in sales.

Director: What's wrong with that?

Model: Customers won't be buying the product. They'll be buying me!

Director: They'll be buying both you and the product. So find a product you can feel good about.

Model: I don't know what that would be.

Director: What's something you love?

Model: Animals.

Director: Then sell products that have to do with them. And if you're unhappy that people are buying because of you, be happy that the animals do well.

Model: There is a veterinary clinic I'd like to help.

Director: Then help them.

Model: It can't pay much.

Director: I thought you saved up money from your modeling career.

Model: I did.

Director: Then what's the problem?

Model: I guess there is no problem. But what about you?

Director: What about me?

Model: Are you happy with what you do?

Director: What do you think I do?

Model: You run operations at a corporation.

Director: That's how I make my money. But what do I do?

Model: Have conversations like this.

Director: And who do you think they help?

Model: The conversations? Those you talk to.

Director: Maybe. But who they definitely help is me.

Model: But you know your conversations help others!

Director: At best I suspect they're important to them.

Model: Nonsense. Judging from myself, I know they help. But I've always had a suspicion.

Director: What suspicion?

Model: You only talk to me because of my looks.

Director: There are many good looking men in the world. I don't talk to them all.

Model: Then why me?

Director: Because you care enough to ask.

~ POPULAR

Model: Why do you think I care?

Director: Because you're suspicious of your looks.

Model: What are you suspicious of?

Director: Your looks.

Model: Ha! But really.

Director: I'm suspicious of what I think of myself.

Model: We have that in common. How can we get over our suspicions?

Director: We can define ourselves very clearly to ourselves.

Model: Until then what are we? The undefined?

Director: We are what we do. And what we do is seek to define.

Model: What happens if we come to define ourselves?

Director: No more suspicions? Just knowledge? We'll celebrate, what else?

Model: Do you think others define themselves with ease?

Director: I think they settle for external definitions.

Model: What does that mean?

Director: It means if someone is willing to pay you a million dollars because of how you look, you define yourself that way. But it can also mean you define yourself by, for instance, the brands you wear.

Model: Clothing, cars, and so on?

Director: Yes, of course. Why do you think people are willing to pay so much for these things? Who needs a car that goes 200 miles per hour when the speed limit is 65?

Model: I have one of those cars. And I have the clothing, too.

Director: Yes, but you want something more.

Model: So do the others I know who own those things.

Director: Really? But don't they just settle for more and better things?

Model: I think you have a point.

Director: What do you really want?

Model: Something I've wanted since I met you.

Director: What?

Model: To be the most beautiful philosopher there has ever been.

Director: All philosophers are beautiful in their way. But you're talking about the beauty of the body, the form, the superficial looks.

Model: Yes.

Director: Hmm.

Model: Hmm what?

Director: That poses great risks.

Model: Why?

Director: Philosophers must avoid unwanted attention. You, to put it mildly, would have a problem with that.

Model: What do philosophers do to avoid the attention? Make themselves boring, as you were saying?

Director: For one, yes. But, Model, you would have a hard time with that.

Model: Why?

Director: Because people will, because of your looks, be excited by you.

Model: You have a point. But why must philosophers avoid attention?

Director: Unwanted attention. Because philosophers are always at risk.

Model: Risk of what?

Director: Being condemned.

Model: For what? The truth?

Director: The unpopular truth.

Model: So philosophy is really just counterculture.

Director: Culture and popularity are different things.

Model: Yes, but philosophy is countercultural and unpopular at once.

Director: Then you're going to have a problem.

Model: Why?

Director: I think you might do well as a figure of a counterculture. Many good looking people end up there. But looks, my friend, are popular—like it or not.

- ~ REBELLION, COMFORT, IDEALS

Model: So what can I do?

Director: In order to rebel? What have the rebellious beautiful of the countercultures always done?

Model: Thumbed their nose at the dominant culture.

Director: But philosophers can ill afford that stunt.

Model: Why?

Director: Because when the good looking of the counterculture act that way, people write them off as immature, whatever. But if a philosopher acts that way? There's real trouble here.

Model: Because the philosopher is a threat.

Director: Yes, philosophy is a threat.

Model: To what? The majority?

Director: No, it's not that simple. And it's not simply a threat to the dominant culture, though it is such a threat. Philosophy is a threat to comfort.

Model: Are you serious?

Director: I am.

Model: Well, then it's no threat to me. I'm not comfortable in the least.

Director: Who is comfortable in this world?

Model: Let's start with who isn't. Philosophers.

Director: If that's true, why would anyone want to be a philosopher?

Model: Because if you have to be uncomfortable, you may as well make others uncomfortable, too.

Director: And that's all philosophy is?

Model: No, it has to be more.

Director: Why?

Model: Because philosophy is noble.

Director: What is nobility?

Model: Nobility involves high moral principles or ideals.

Director: Is that what you want?

Model: Yes.

Director: Do you already have these principles and ideals?

Model: I do, though I'm sure I could improve in living up to them.

Director: Don't you know?

Model: Know what?

Director: The many can help you with this.

Model: How so?

Director: They like nothing better than elevating people of principle and ideal.

Model: That's not true. If it were true, our crop of politicians would be replaced.

Director: I didn't say they get what they want. I'm saying what they want.

Model: And I might help them get what they want? How can I pull it off?

Director: All it takes is being true to your ideals—and putting yourself forward to the crowd. I think I can help you here.

- Beliefs, Philosophy

Model: Where should we begin?

Director: We have to articulate your ideals. So what do you believe?

Model: I... don't know.

Director: What do you mean you don't know?

Model: I've never thought this through!

Director: But you said you already have them.

Model: I'm sure I do... somewhere.

Director: And you'd like to be a philosopher.

Model: I'm sorry! Help me, please.

Director: Let's forget for now what you believe, and let's focus on what you want to believe.

Model: I like that approach. I want to believe I can make a difference.

Director: What kind of difference?

Model: A positive one.

Director: You want to make the world a better place?

Model: I do.

Director: For whom?

Model: Everyone? Do you think that's possible?

Director: I don't know. I usually have a more narrow focus.

Model: How do you want to change the world?

Director: I want to secure a future for philosophy.

Model: That's a narrow focus?

Director: More narrow—and therefore more likely to succeed. But then again, nothing could be more broad.

Model: How so?

Director: Don't you think philosophy has the most comprehensive view of the world?

Model: I do. But some might say the view is nothing unless action follows.

Director: Philosophy acts. It tries to bring more philosophers into the world.

Model: By 'bring' do you mean something like create? In other words, philosophy breeds philosophy?

Director: Is there anything strange in that?

Model: But what's the goal of philosophy? I mean, we could have a million philosophers—but what are they supposed to do?

Director: Knock down the false ideals.

Model: What if an ideal is true but the person purporting to hold it is false?

Director: We might as well knock them down, too.

Model: I think I like this sort of philosophy.

Director: Would you like it as your ideal?

Model: I would. After all, I want the world to be a better place.

- PHILOSOPHERS, POPULAR THOUGHT, EFFORT

Director: You know, there will never be a million philosophers—not unless the human population grows exponentially for a great long while.

Model: Why not? Is there some sort of ratio you have in mind?

Director: Not a ratio, exactly. But it seems to me that the number of philosophers will always be relatively small.

Model: Why?

Director: It's very hard to escape popular thought.

Model: That's true. But I'm surprised you call it thought.

Director: Popular thought exists in a narrow band of the true. So it can be truthful, but incomplete.

Model: But often times it's not even truthful.

Director: That's true. And often times it's not even thought.

Model: What is it?

Director: Opinions generated from deeply held beliefs.

Model: And philosophers want to swap those opinions for truths?

Director: Yes.

Model: I could do that.

Director: I'm not so sure.

Model: Why?

Director: Because of your looks.

Model: I don't see how that's relevant.

Director: There are two things you have to consider. One, there are people who will listen to you because of your looks. Do you know why that's a problem?

Model: Because it's likely they're not listening very well. What's the second thing?

Director: There are those who see how this goes on who will refuse to believe anything you say out of a sort of disgust.

Model: Disgust because they think it comes so easy to me? Well, it makes me think of the opposite case.

Director: Oh?

Model: A friend and I were watching the news, and an ugly reporter came on. My friend said, 'Boy, she must be a really good reporter if she can be that ugly and still succeed.'

Director: Do you think your friend had a point?

Model: Yes, I do.

Director: If you head down the path of philosophy, you're going to have to try as hard as that reporter.

Model: Do you think I'm afraid of hard work?

Director: Have you worked hard before?

Model: A day on a shoot is no piece of cake.

Director: What's hard about it?

Model: It's exhausting to do what you're told.

Director: Do you think philosophers do what they're told?

Model: I... don't.

- As Good As They Can

Director: Not even in universities?

Model: No one tells university philosophers what to do.

Director: No? Then maybe it's just understood.

Model: Understood what they must do.

Director: Yes.

Model: But how would a philosophy professor know what's understood?

Director: He or she bumps up against it and knows.

Model: Do you think many buck the system?

Director: Some do. But many fear what happens if they go against it.

Model: What happens is they never get tenure. Never become part of the system.

Director: Are you part of a system, Model?

Model: I don't know about that. People just tell me to do certain things because they're trying to make me look as good as I can.

Director: Professors, too, want to look as good as they can.

Model: Everyone wants to look as good as they can. How do professors do it?

Director: One of the ways is the peer review of their writings.

Model: Yes, but the purpose of the review is to ensure the author is telling the truth.

Director: Truth doesn't make them look good?

Model: Of course it does—unless it's 'truth' and not truth.

Director: An understood 'truth'.

Model: Yes.

Director: Do you have experience with anything like this?

Model: I guess 'truth' in my world is when my images are enhanced.

Director: Enhanced?

Model: To make me look leaner, more muscular, more... perfect.

Director: I think that's a mistake. There is no perfect when it comes to looks.

Model: I'm with you. But many people don't see it that way.

Director: Are these the same many who would gladly engineer perfect looking children for themselves?

Model: I think they are.

Director: Will there be competing notions of perfect among them?

Model: Yes, but only so many. There will be a tendency toward a small number of types.

Director: I think we need flourishing countercultures of looks.

Model: For the sake of diversity.

Director: Yes. How do you think we can support them?

Model: We don't engineer our children, and we love them for however they look.

Director: How about just a little engineering, to make them healthier?

Model: I suppose that's fine. Health is one thing; looks is another.

Director: Some would say health is beauty.

Model: There's truth in that. And looks on their own are no prize.

Director: Talk like that you and might be a hero to the cause.

Model: I'd rather be that than what I am now.

Director: What's wrong with what you are now?

Model: No one takes me seriously.

Director: I find that hard to believe. I'm sure there are millions of teenagers who take how you look very seriously.

Model: I want them to take me seriously for something more.

Director: What?

Model: My mind!

Director: What about your mind?

Model: The thoughts I have.

Director: What kind of thoughts do you have?

Model: We're talking about them now!

Director: Do you want them to take you seriously as a philosopher?

Model: Yes.

Director: Do you think philosophers are generally taken seriously?

Model: Maybe not generally.

Director: A minority takes philosophers seriously?

Model: Yes, a minority. An important minority.

Director: No doubt. Why do you think they take philosophy seriously?

Model: Because they know something is wrong.

Director: Something is wrong?

Model: With the world.

Director: But plenty of people think there's something wrong with the world, and they have no love for philosophy. Is there a particular wrong you have in mind?

~ APPEARANCES

Model: Appearances.

Director: What do you mean?

Model: People are taken with appearances and they ignore the truth inside.

Director: And you're not just talking about what happens to models.

Model: No, it happens to everyone. Everyone every single day. People judge by appearances, and it's a crime.

Director: They judge other people? Or do they also judge situations and so on?

Model: Yes, people and situations—all on how they appear.

Director: You'd like it if people's judgment were improved.

Model: I'd like them to focus on truth and not appearances.

Director: How do you think we can help them do that?

Model: For most people, I think it's a hopeless cause. But for a certain minority, much can be done.

Director: How?

Model: These people have a hunger for truth. We feed them.

Director: Do they have a hunger for all truth, or for certain truths?

Model: Well, that's a hard question. I suppose very few people want all the truth. Most just want what they want to hear.

Director: Have you noticed that some desperately want to hear about what they see?

Model: What, do you mean they want someone to make sense of it for them? Yes, I've noticed. And I think it's pathetic. Why can't they trust their own eyes?

Director: Because what they see goes against what they believe. It's a sort of blindness. And it's especially pronounced concerning the inner qualities of others.

Model: They misjudge the good.

Director: And the bad. After all, they sometimes praise the ugly inside who happen to have good looks.

Model: They just can't see the inner ugly even when it's right in their face.

Director: It happens all the time.

Model: I hate it.

Director: Why?

Model: Because it's unjust!

Director: Do you think you deserve some praise?

Model: I might. But I don't want it for the wrong reasons. And I get it all the time.

Director: That really bothers you, doesn't it?

Model: Immensely.

Director: You're unusual here. Most people, I think, take praise wherever they can get it.   But I want friends like you.

Model: Good looking friends?

Director: Sure, that's no crime.

Model: Ha! Look at you grin. That's not really what you want.

Director: No, I want friends—however they look.

Model: But what kind of friends do you want?

Director: The kind that has an interest in philosophy.

Model: You want philosophers as friends?

Director: I prefer to admire fully fledged philosophers from afar.

Model: Why?

Director: Because I like diversity in my set.

- Sets, The Best, Liberation

Model: I don't really have a set.

Director: That makes you unusual among models, no?

Model: All my peers have their set within the scene.

Director: The scene?

Model: Model land.

Director: Are you saying you traverse model land alone?

Model: I think you're teasing, but the answer is yes.

Director: I think that makes you unique. And I'll tell you something more.

Model: Please.

Director: It wouldn't be possible if you weren't the best looking model around.

Model: Thanks. I think you have a point. They wouldn't put up with me if I weren't.

Director: Why did you thank me just now?

Model: That's a really good question. I thanked you because you paid me a standard compliment. I shouldn't have thanked you. You complimented me on something I can't help.

Director: Don't you have to diet and work out in order to stay in shape?

Model: I'll let you in on a secret. I eat and drink whatever I like, and don't work out that hard.

Director: So you feel you don't deserve the praise.

Model: And it's not even really praise. I'm the best looking model around. That's a descriptive statement. And we might say there are a few who are equally good looking. So we might say there are none more attractive than me, and that would be just. But it's not my doing. It just is. We might say the same about you.

Director: I'm the best looking?

Model: Ha, ha. No. There's no philosopher more... what?

Director: Philosophical than me?

Model: Yes. None are more philosophical than Director.

Director: I don't know that.

Model: But I do. It's true!

Director: If it's true, it sounds like a terrible responsibility. But am I like you? It's just what I am and it can't be helped?

Model: Most of your friends would deny it, and say you deserve praise for intrepid thought, and so on. But I don't think the way they think. I think your philosophical-ness is just like my looks. It can't be helped.

Director: I'm stunned. You're the first person to tell me this. And I find it somewhat... liberating!

Model: So neither of us deserves the praise we get. How can we deserve it?

Director: I'll be more like you and you'll be more like me?

Model: Yes!

Director: But hold on. You can become more like me by practicing philosophy. But how am I supposed to become more like you? No matter what I do I'll never have your looks.

Model: You just don't want to eat right and train very hard.

Director: And you don't want to study abstruse passages from great philosophers. Or do you?

Model: I'm willing to do what it takes.

Director: But what if I tell you to save yourself the headaches and just talk to me?

Model: Are you offering a shortcut? Or do you just want me in your set?

Director: My set of friends? Yes. A shortcut? No, I'll work you hard. But I won't give you headaches.

Model: Why not?

Director: Because people get headaches when they feel there must be a point they just can't grasp. I will show you the point every time.

Model: So you'll leave no work to me?

Director: Oh no. I will leave plenty of work to you. Because the point is just the beginning.

- WHAT PHILOSOPHY IS

Model: So what's the most important point?

Director: Concerning looks? They matter.

Model: Ha!

Director: You laugh, but I know something about you.

Model: What do you know?

Director: That you wish they didn't.

Model: I've told you as much just now.

Director: Yes, but you really wish they didn't. You're uncomfortable with your looks. That's the reason you have no set. And that's the reason you're flirting with philosophy.

Model: Why do you think I'm just flirting?

Director: Did you ever want to know something so badly you stayed up all night to figure it out?

Model: Well, no. Did you?

Director: Yes. On numerous occasions I stayed up with friends to work things through.

Model: I wish I had friends like that.

Director: It's a shame you don't. Longing for conversation is a sign of philosophy.

Model: But it's not enough?

Director: Of course it's not enough.

Model: What does it take?

Director: Do you want me to lie or tell you the truth?

Model: Why would I want you to lie?

Director: Because you'll be familiar with the lie. It's what most would-be philosophers say.

Model: What do they say?

Director: That the point of philosophy is truth, that the philosopher experiences a longing for truth.

Model: Isn't that what the philosopher experiences?

Director: Yes and no. It would take a very long conversation to tease the meaning out here.

Model: What's the bottom line?

Director: Philosophy isn't a longing for truth.

Model: Is philosophy a longing?

Director: Yes, but it's also an act.

Model: You mean it's fake?

Director: No. Philosophy does more than long. It acts on its longing.

Model: Oh, I see. What's the act in question?

Director: The destruction of false belief.

Model: Through reason?

Director: Yes.

Model: What's a false belief?

Director: For instance? You believe you're God's gift to the world.

Model: You know I don't believe that.

Director: Yes, but others believe it of you.

Model: So if I'm a philosopher, I have to set out to destroy their false belief in me.

Director: That would be a good first step.

Model: And the first step is to reason with them?

Director: Ah, you're more of a philosopher than I thought.

Model: What makes you say that?

Director: You have a sense for the limitation of reason. Otherwise you would never say reason is just the first step.

Model: So philosophers destroy false beliefs through other means. What means?

Director: Through every means at their disposal.

- DESTRUCTION, CONSTRUCTION

Model: I've learned a little about philosophy, you know.

Director: What did you learn?

Model: That there are two kinds of philosophy—destructive and constructive.

Director: Did you learn you must clear the ground before you build?

Model: Yes.

Director: And what kind of buildings should philosophy erect?

Model: Useful buildings.

Director: Temples to house beautiful people?

Model: Be serious.

Director: I am. Philosophers are beautiful, you know.

Model: Would you really live in a temple?

Director: If it were a comfortable temple? I would. Would you?

Model: You're talking about a temple for physically beautiful people?

Director: Do you doubt philosophers are physically beautiful?

Model: Are you talking about the brain? Well, of course. But philosophers' beauty is in the soul, Director.

Director: You want there to be more than the physical.

Model: I do. Don't you?

Director: I go back and forth on this quite a bit.

Model: Why? Isn't it bleak to think there's nothing more than the physical?

Director: Roses are physical. The scent of the rose is physical. The pleasure I feel when I sniff is physical.

Model: Yes, but you're not taking into account the sublime.

Director: What if I tell you the sublime is nothing more than a complex combination of physical effects?

Model: I'd ask you to prove it.

Director: I'd ask you to prove the sublime exists.

Model: You know it when you feel it. There is no proof.

Director: Do philosophers experience the sublime?

Model: I think they do—when they are constructing beautiful theories. What else could motivate them?

Director: What if they're constructing one theory simply in order to knock down another?

Model: So what do they do? Build and destroy, build and destroy?

Director: I don't know, Model. I keep trying to build but I fail miserably.

Model: What have you tried to build?

Director: Honestly? A temple to myself.

Model: Why did you fail?

Director: Because I wasn't worthy.

Model: Why weren't you worthy?

Director: I didn't believe in my own beauty.

Model: I can help you with that.

Director: You can make me believe I'm beautiful?

Model: You yourself said philosophers are beautiful. And you're a philosopher.

Director: You have a point. But maybe I'm a very bad philosopher.

Model: How do you think you might get better?

Director: I think I know how many would-be philosophers would try to get better. They'd try to get other people to believe in their beauty. And then, with this to lend them courage, they might start to believe in their beauty themselves. But I'm sure you can't understand this.

Model: Why do you say that?

Director: Because you've never had to try to get anyone to believe in your beauty.

- BELIEF

Model: How do you know I don't encounter people who think I'm just another dumb model? They're not impressed.

Director: I think you open your mouth and something happens. They start to believe.

Model: What do they believe?

Director: That you're not just another dumb model.

Model: Many models aren't dumb, you know.

Director: I believe it.

Model: People want to believe they're dumb.

Director: Why do you think that is?

Model: It's a sort of revenge.

Director: Revenge on their beauty?

Model: Yes.

Director: No one is allowed to have it all. Is that it?

Model: That's exactly it.

Director: So you have a beautiful body. You're smart. And you want to be a philosopher. People are sure to hate you.

Model: Ha, ha.

Director: How can you tell when people believe in you?

Model: There's a sort of feeling you get.

Director: Can you describe it?

Model: It's a sort of chemistry you feel.

Director: Are you talking about love?

Model: Love and belief are closely aligned in the heart.

Director: Can you love someone you don't believe in?

Model: When you stop believing you fall out of love.

Director: If you fall out of love does that mean the belief was bad?

Model: I never thought about it that way before. But I suppose that's how it is.

Director: So philosophers would seek to destroy this bad belief.

Model: Philosophers would really seek to make people fall out of love?

Director: What do you think?

Model: I think it's a great idea. How many people fall in love with me for the wrong reasons?

Director: Many?

Model: Of course many! If you could free me of them I'd be grateful.

Director: I must confess. I've never been offered a job like this before. How do you think I'd do it?

Model: You'd tell them the truth about me.

Director: No, that won't do.

Model: Why not?

Director: Because that might make them fall in love more deeply!

Model: But then it would be true love.

Director: Are you forgetting true love requires reciprocation?

Model: But why shouldn't I love those who love me for the right reasons?

Director: They'd love you for being a philosopher?

Model: Yes. Philosophy is a noble calling.

Director: And it's right to love the noble?

Model: Of course.

Director: How do we know something is noble as opposed to believing it's noble?

Model: You can feel it.

Director: I thought you feel it either way.

Model: You do. But when you know it, you really feel it.

Director: How do you know philosophy is noble, aside from feeling?

Model: Philosophy does a service for people. Yes?

Director: In getting rid of bad love? Yes.

Model: It's good to do a good service.

Director: It is.

Model: Philosophy does this service for free. Right?

Director: True.

Model: That, to me, Director, is the definition of noble. A good service for others done for free.

Director: It's hard to argue with that.

Model: Then don't.

~ Falling Out of Love

Director: But is it really free?

Model: Do you charge like a therapist would?

Director: No, but that raises an interesting point. Can therapists make people fall out of love?

Model: No.

Director: Then how can philosophers?

Model: They can't always. I mean, if you're head over heels in love, you're not going to listen to anyone who tells you the love is wrong, the love is untrue.

Director: Love is blind.

Model: Yes, and when it is, the love usually isn't reciprocated.

Director: True. Aside from that, what's the problem here?

Model: Aside from being blind and alone in your love? The real problem is when the beloved plays on your love.

Director: Plays on your love?

Model: They take advantage.

Director: You mean they encourage the lover to buy them expensive gifts?

Model: Sure, things like that. And there are many other ways to take advantage.

Director: Name one.

Model: The beloved wants the lover to feed their ego.

Director: And feeding an ego isn't cheap.

Model: I can't tell if you're being serious or not, but it's true. It takes a psychological toll.

Director: Can you say more about this toll?

Model: The lover lowers her- or himself in order to lift the beloved higher.

Director: Hmm. Couldn't the lover go higher and pull the beloved up?

Model: I suppose you have a point. That's possible.

Director: In that case, what's the cost to the lover?

Model: It's not easy to pull someone else up. It's exhausting to carry that weight.

Director: And when they're beyond exhausted I suppose there's guilt.

Model: What do you mean?

Director: Might the lover not feel guilty about, finally, cutting ties?

Model: There's a good chance they might.

Director: Have you ever lifted someone up?

Model: I haven't. Have you?

Director: No, but not for lack of opportunity.

Model: Do you often fall in love with those beneath you?

Director: I don't like the metaphor anymore. Perhaps I'd say they're like a great big hot air balloon, and I'm on the ground trying to pull them down. It's hopeless.

Model: So you just let them float away?

Director: Well, I have to admit—I do carry a slingshot with me for such occasions. A little rock shot well can deflate them a bit and bring them gently down to earth.

Model: Or it might tear a gaping hole and send them crashing down to earth.

Director: Now I'm not liking this metaphor, either.

Model: Then let's try to think of one you like.

- METAPHORS OR NOT

Director: The problem with metaphors is that they involve talking about something while not talking about that thing.

Model: The good thing about metaphors is that they help you get at difficult things.

Director: True. Let's think of a metaphor for looks.

Model: I'd like to hear one from you, because the topic is a little too close to home for me.

Director: Alright. Looks are like....

Model: What's wrong?

Director: I'm at a loss. I can't think what looks are like.

Model: Oh, just say anything and we'll work it through.

Director: Looks are like.... I can't bring myself to say just anything about such an important topic.

Model: Now I think you're teasing. Then I'll say something. Forget metaphors. Let's say what looks are.

Director: I'm eagerly awaiting your words.

Model: Looks are a thing we wish we had.

Director: You mean good looks are a thing we wish we had.

Model: Yes, of course. Everyone has a look. Only some of us have good looks.

Director: And even fewer have great looks. So what does that mean? Great looks are a thing we wish we had? It's a sort of envy when we encounter those with great looks? Attraction to them means we want what they have?

Model: Yes.

Director: But many people are attracted to the opposite sex. Does this mean men long to have the looks of the women they love, and the other way round?

Model: I'm going to be bold and say yes.

Director: People will think we're crazy, talking like this.

Model: We're only telling the truth.

Director: Maybe it would be better to say lovers long to be a match, a counterpart, to the one they love.

Model: That makes sense.

Director: But, nonetheless, people wish they looked like you.

Model: Or could be my counterpart in looks, yes.

Director: Maybe some of them simply wish you loved them for how they look right now.

Model: Well, I suppose if I did I'd validate their looks.

Director: That's it? That's all that would happen?

Model: Director, let me tell you. Love to me is of the heart and soul.

Director: And not the mind?

Model: Heart, mind, soul—yes.

Director: I think you could find many people who would say they love you for those things.

Model: Sure, but I want someone who means it.

Director: You want the love of your life.

Model: Of course I do. Doesn't everyone?

Director: Some people want more than one love in their life.

Model: In the course of their life? Do you?

Director: Well, it's funny you ask. I've been giving this some thought. I don't think I do.

Model: Why not?

Director: Because I've noticed that when people leave one love, it often involves a terrible wrenching of the gut.

Model: The gut or the heart?

Director: I think it's a little of both.

Model: And it's only sometimes?

Director: Usually, let's say.

Model: Who are the unusual here?

Director: Let's not get sidetracked. This wrenching, it discourages people from trying new love.

Model: So what are you suggesting? That people believe in the love of their life because they're afraid to try new love?

Director: I would be a fool to suggest something like that. But it's many times probably true.

- TRUE LOVE, SOUL

Model: All I can say is that I have a longing, a great desire for the love of my life.

Director: Beliefs give shape to longings and desires.

Model: To give shape is different than to cause.

Director: Certainly.

Model: Would you give my desire a different shape?

Director: All I'm suggesting is that you take love for what it is, and be open to better love.

Model: But you have to make a commitment. 'This is who I love.'

Director: I'm sorry. Was that to the point?

Model: Wasn't it?

Director: Can you repeat what you said?

Model: You have to commit to your love. For good.

Director: Yes, and how well does that go for most people?

Model: Most? Not... so good.

Director: If love is true, why do you have to commit? The love sustains itself. Ask any true lovers. They'll agree.

Model: I guess you have a point. But let me ask you this. Can love be sustained by looks?

Director: I think it can. But I'm not talking about conventional good looks. I mean something like this—'I just like the way you look.'

Model: And others might think you look ugly; but it wouldn't matter, because I like the way you look.

Director: Yes.

Model: But what about character?

Director: It follows from looks.

Model: That's a big lie.

Director: Where does character come from?

Model: The heart, the soul.

Director: Where do the heart and soul come from?

Model: They just... are!

Director: If you want to be a philosopher, you'll have to do better than that.

Model: Do you really think looks shape heart and soul?

Director: I do. Not solely, of course. But they have a hand.

Model: How?

Director: When shaping the soul, there are two inputs. One from without, and one from within.

Model: What do they amount to?

Director: They tell you what you are.

Model: Which should you believe?

Director: That, my friend, is an excellent philosophical question.

Model: Why?

Director: Because it expresses a profound doubt—both of yourself and of others.

Model: So what's the answer?

Director: Dialogue.

Model: I knew you'd say that.

Director: But it's true. You must place the internal and external voices into a reasoned dialogue and see what prevails.

Model: And this truth can differ from both the internal and external voices?

Director: Of course.

Model: But it, ultimately, has to be from my own voice. I'm the one thinking here.

Director: But, Model, don't you know?

Model: Know what?

Director: The voice can be an instrument played by a wonderful player.

Model: And what's the name of this player?

Director: Philosophy.

- Philosophy, Politics

Model: I'm not so sure I want to be 'played'.

Director: Think of it this way. Suppose you were a beautifully made violin. Wouldn't you want to be played? And before you answer, I would like to say that you are more beautiful than a beautiful violin.

Model: I see you like to flatter. But if I truly am like a violin? Yes, I'd like to be played. But only by a master violinist.

Director: Well, you're in luck—because I'm a master philosopher.

Model: Ha! I see modesty doesn't enter into your thought.

Director: It took me a long time to decide that I am what I am. So please don't make light of what I say.

Model: So play me, then.

Director: That's what I've been doing—as you've been playing me.

Model: Do you really mean it? Do you think I'm a philosopher?

Director: If you are, we need to protect you.

Model: From what?

Director: Jealousy. No one can have it all. You're trying to fly very close to the sun.

Model: So what should I give up? Philosophy?

Director: You know I wouldn't recommend that lightly. But how can you give up your looks?

Model: You see my dilemma.

Director: Yes. Hmm. I guess there's nothing to it but to be bold.

Model: Maybe I should just stop modeling.

Director: What would you do?

Model: Maybe I'll go into law.

Director: No!

Model: Why do you object so strongly?

Director: Because law will lead you, in particular, to politics.

Model: What's wrong with that? People will vote for me because of my looks.

Director: But you'll have to give up philosophy.

Model: Who says I'll have to?

Director: Politics is about getting people to believe.

Model: But that's just it. I'll construct. And don't worry, I'll seek to get rid of the bad ideas in the electorate, too. Both sides of philosophy, all the time. I'll love it.

~ Loving It

Model: Why didn't I think of this sooner?

Director: Yes, why didn't you?

Model: Because I felt that law school would expose me as a fraud.

Director: A fraud?

Model: Unable to think for myself.

Director: How did you get through college?

Model: I took courses graded on papers, and I had friends write the papers.

Director: Sounds like good practice for politics.

Model: But you can understand why I had doubts about law. In law school you have to read the assigned cases and then summarize them when called on in class.

Director: Did the thought of that make you nervous?

Model: Yes, of course.

Director: What made you nervous? The reading and summarizing, or the presentation?

Model: Not the presentation.

Director: You could have joined a study group where you write the summaries with friends. I hear they do these sorts of things.

Model: But I would have been the weak link. People would only ask me to join their group because of my looks. And then I'd be a disappointment to them.

Director: Is that your greatest fear? Disappointing?

Model: It is. I don't want to let anyone down.

Director: Why not?

Model: What do you mean, 'Why not?'

Director: People who expect good looks to equate to good work are fools.

Model: I couldn't agree more.

Director: Yes, but why did you think you wouldn't be any good?

Model: I never had to apply myself that way. I always got by on looks.

Director: Your looks were a sort of crutch?

Model: Yes, exactly.

Director: And you wish you could throw away the crutch. Maybe politics really is best for you.

Model: You think so? Why?

Director: It will force you to walk.

Model: How? I'll make speeches written by others. I'll shake hands with people who love me for how I look.

Director: Yes, but think of the journalists. They, and their audience, will want something more.

Model: What will they want?

Director: To know where you stand on all the issues of the day,

Model: I can have my team tell me where I stand. Then I just have to remember.

Director: Are you okay with that?

Model: I am.

Director: Would you call this standing on your own two feet?

Model: I'll stand the way an actor stands. We've had actor politicians before.

Director: And the things you'll make the electorate believe, they'll come from your staff?

Model: Why not?

Director: And the beliefs you'll destroy?

Model: I'd rather arrive at those on my own. And maybe you can help.

    - Helping

Director: Spoken like a true politician. 'I'll come up with them all on my own, but I'd like you to help.'

Model: Not even philosophers operate in complete isolation, Director. You know that.

Director: Of course I do, Model. But when we think, we always think alone.

Model: We as in all of us? Or we as in we philosophers?

Director: We philosophers.

Model: Why don't the rest of us think alone?

Director: We use the voices of others as crutches.

Model: Can you say more?

Director: When we think about a problem in our lives, we lean on what others have said before.

Model: Others we admire?

Director: Yes. Your father, for instance, might have told you something once about a similar problem, and so you grasp on to what he said and use it to 'solve' your problem for you. And so on and so on.

Model: What's wrong with that?

Director: You're not really thinking. You're remembering and using those memories to guide you.

Model: Maybe these memories are like training wheels. You use them until you get up on your own.

Director: I like that better. Even philosophers at one point had training wheels.

Model: Other philosophers?

Director: Yes. They keep them around for a while until they're ready to move on.

Model: And what do they do? Just abandon them?

Director: I'll put it this way for effect. Philosophers go from deep reverence for to simple admiration of other philosophers.

Model: Do all philosophers go through this transition?

Director: I don't know.

Model: Did you?

Director: Yes.

Model: Who did you revere? And when?

Director: I revered one ancient and one modern. I read Plato when I was a boy and that persuaded me toward philosophy. But then I read Strauss when I was in college, and that changed things for me.

Model: How did they change?

Director: Strauss wrote about Plato and suggested that everything wasn't as it seemed.

Model: So you went and took a second look at Plato?

Director: Yes.

Model: What did you find?

Director: That everything wasn't as it seemed.

Model: So what did you do?

Director: I tried following Strauss's interpretation of the Athenian.

Model: And?

Director: I found it impossible to follow.

Model: Why?

Director: Because Plato taught me something as I read.

- SECRET KNOWLEDGE, DIALOGUE

Model: What did Plato teach you?

Director: How to read Strauss.

Model: What did Plato say?

Director: There was no way Strauss was as serious as he let on.

Model: I never read him. Why did he seem so serious?

Director: Oh, his reasoning, his sentences, his themes. They added up to a thicket of seriousness that serious students mostly never got through.

Model: He attracted serious students with his reasoning and so on?

Director: Yes, he did.

Model: What makes someone become a serious student?

Director: It's hard to say. But I think they feel there's something to be gained.

Model: What?

Director: Knowledge of the themselves and the world.

Model: Wouldn't it be better to gain that knowledge in the world rather than at a study desk?

Director: One would think so, yes. But then there's the secret knowledge.

Model: What secret knowledge?

Director: This was one of Strauss's themes.

Model: What was the secret knowledge?

Director: He never said. He just claimed that philosophers write in such a way to conceal the knowledge in question.

Model: Did you figure out what the secret knowledge is?

Director: I did.

Model: What is it? You have to tell me now.

Director: It has to do with what philosophy is.

Model: What is philosophy?

Director: I don't have a simple answer for you friend, even though I talk about philosophy all the time.

Model: Why not?

Director: It's a secret.

Model: Ha! What is it? What is philosophy? It's not love of knowledge.

Director: No, it's not—though knowledge is very important here.

Model: Is it truthfulness, radical truthfulness?

Director: That goes hand-in-hand with knowledge, but is still not it.

Model: Love of wisdom?

Director: Yes, but no.

Model: The desire to build up true opinions and beliefs, and tear down the false?

Director: Yes, but not quite that.

Model: I give up. What's the secret?

Director: It can't be said in so many words. It has to become clear through dialogue. On the one hand, when we dialogue, we're discussing the issue at hand. On the other hand, we are showing, demonstrating, what philosophy is. Over time the secret becomes clear to those who listen with care.

Model: So you're recommending I spend lots of time with you.

Director: Yes, I am.

Model: Then sign me up.

~ TECHNIQUE, RESPECT

Director: But now I feel ridiculous.

Model: Why?

Director: There is no secret to philosophy. All you have to do is watch and see. It's like saying there's a secret to football. Sure, there are techniques that aren't obvious to the untrained eye; but football is football; just as philosophy is philosophy.

Model: I want to learn all the techniques from you.

Director: But that's the thing. I can teach you my techniques. But they won't work for you.

Model: Why not?

Director: Techniques are designed with one particular philosopher in mind.

Model: Who designs them?

Director: The philosopher. But sometimes...

Model: Sometimes what?

Director: ...another philosopher makes a suggestion, gives a little hint, that goes a very long way.

Model: Give me a suggestion, Director.

Director: You have to decide what kind of philosopher you want to be. Will you be one who never forgets his looks, or will you be one who always forgets his looks?

Model: Why not shoot for the middle? I'll remember and forget when appropriate.

Director: Don't you want to be consistent in your philosophy?

Model: Oh. I wasn't thinking of that.

Director: You don't have to be consistent, you know.

Model: No, but I'd like to be. People don't take me seriously as it is now. How do you think they'll take me if I'm inconsistent?

Director: So what will you do? Remember or forget your looks?

Model: I will remember them always, because of the effect they'll have on most. But I'll play them down. If people see I don't value my looks more highly than my mind, they might come to respect me and treat me the way I want.

Director: Is respect really what you want?

Model: I think it is. I get plenty of admiration for my looks. But I wouldn't say people respect me because of them. Respect is something more.

Director: What is respect?

Model: It has to do with power. In this case, the power of the mind.

Director: Those who respect you treat as you as at least an equal in this power?

Model: Exactly.

Director: Hmm.

Model: What is it?

Director: It's just something I've been mulling over, something about power.

Model: Tell me.

Director: Someone once told me that power is more attractive than looks. And the attraction is the same sort of attraction. Chemistry, strong chemistry you can feel. What do you think?

Model: I think you just gave up your secret, the secret to philosophy. It wants power, and it wants this power to be recognized and loved. What do you think?

Director: I've never thought about it this way before. I'll have to take some time to think it through.

Model: Then are you saying I'm wrong about the secret?

Director: No, I'm saying *I* may be wrong about the secret. I need to think it through.

Model: Think it through with me.

Director: Well, let's start with this. Are we saying love and recognition and respect amount to roughly the same thing?

Model: For purposes of discussion, we can say that. So let's just stick with love.

- LOVE, FALLEN RIDERS

Director: Does everyone want love?

Model: Everyone who's living, yes.

Director: So everyone has certain things they do, they try, in order to secure love.

Model: Well, now we're complicating things. They do what they do in order to have love, not necessarily secure it.

Director: Do you want love you can't secure?

Model: It's better than no love.

Director: True. Now, you get love without even trying. Or are you going to say there are different types of love and you don't get the kind you want?

Model: That's what I'm going to say. I want more from life than that kind of love.

Director: And that's the thing. Most people don't want more from life than that. Love is what they long for; love is what they want— whatever kind of love.

Model: And you're trying to tell me this is what philosophers want in order to discourage me.

Director: No! Philosophers want a very particular kind of love—a love I don't think you have.

Model: And now you're trying to tempt me.

Director: Tempt, discourage—what does it matter? Philosophers want to be loved for what they are.

Model: What are they?

Director: The baddest cowboy in the rodeo.

Model: Ha! What's that supposed to mean?

Director: Do you know who the baddest cowboy in the rodeo is?

Model: Tell me.

Director: The clown who protects the fallen riders.

Model: So now you're telling me philosophers are clowns? And they should be loved for this?

Director: What can I say? I can only go where the dialogue leads.

Model: But you're leading the dialogue!

Director: Am I? I thought we were doing it together.

Model: Clowns aren't easy to love.

Director: Neither are philosophers.

Model: Why not?

Director: Because they're taken with serving the cause.

Model: What cause?

Director: The cause of philosophy, what else?

Model: What is the cause of philosophy?

Director: Its survival.

Model: That's it? That's all philosophy wants? To survive?

Director: Survive and do what it does.

Model: Its secret work, you mean.

Director: Something like that.

- Work, Chance

Model: So what's the work?

Director: Dialogue.

Model: What does that accomplish?

Director: It plows up the fertile field and prepares it for planting.

Model: Are we plowing up the fertile field today?

Director: I think we are. But how good a job we did won't be known for some time.

Model: Like a few days?

Director: Like many years.

Model: Are you really that patient?

Director: No, I try to plow a field as often as I can. You can get better at it that way, you know.

Model: So what will you do? Call me in ten years and see how I'm doing?

Director: I'd rather be friends with you throughout those years so we can enjoy each other's company and maybe make some adjustments along the way.

Model: Suppose you have success. What grows in the field?

Director: I don't know.

Model: What? You don't know? Why go to the trouble to plow?

Director: I like it when things grow.

Model: And any wind-blown seed will do?

Director: Oh, if it's a weed we'll just rip it up. We're looking for vigorous shoots that promise lovely plants and trees.

Model: You don't have to plow a field to plant a tree.

Director: True. The metaphor has its limits.

Model: Why not plan a garden and get exactly what you want?

Director: Why not genetically manufacture humans and get exactly what we want?

Model: Do you really think it's the same sort of thing?

Director: I do, mostly. There has to be a role for chance in life.

Model: Why?

Director: Chance protects philosophy.

Model: I thought philosophers were opposed to chance.

Director: What would make you think that?

Model: Philosophy wants to think everything through, to know. Chance is the opposite of knowledge. Chance is the unknown.

Director: But we can learn from the unknown, from chance—in ways we can't learn when we have things under control.

Model: So philosophy's work is creating an environment for chance?

Director: Yes. That's the secret, Model. Guard it well.

Model: Are you serious? That's the secret?

Director: That's the secret.

Model: What harm is there in my running around telling everyone the secret?

Director: No harm. But people will think you're crazy. The secret protects itself, you see.

Model: But this is an important theory! The Philosophy of Chance! You should teach this in a university!

Director: I'm sure it's been taught before.

Model: Yes, but not by someone like you.

- DIRECTOR

Director: What am I like?

Model: For one, you're very gentle.

Director: I'm sure there are gentle professors out there.

Model: Yes, but you're open to everything.

Director: No I'm not.

Model: What aren't you open to?

Director: Good looking whiners.

Model: Do you think I'm a good looking whiner?

Director: No.

Model: What do you think I am?

Director: Someone who makes me smile.

Model: Why do you smile?

Director: Because you help me do what I like to do.

Model: And what do you like to do?

Director: Explore.

Model: What sorts of things do you explore?

Director: What friendship is. Who my friends are. Who I am.

Model: Who am I?

Director: You are a fighter going against terrible odds. You want to find true friends, friends who love you for more than your looks. You've found one in me. But you should know something.

Model: What?

Director: I appreciate your looks. They're part of who you are. And I appreciate you as a whole.

Model: That's all I want. To be appreciated as a whole. I appreciate you as a whole, too, Director.

Director: I know you do. But I think you have it hard because of your looks. People just can't get beyond them.

Model: Well, who wants 'people' as their friend, anyway?

Director: That's the spirit! But here's the thing. As a model, you can be aloof and have little to do with people. As a politician, that would be a difficult trick to pull off.

Model: Difficult but not impossible?

Director: Not impossible. But very hard.

- Shy, Comfort

Model: How can I stay aloof without giving offense?

Director: You could pretend to be terribly shy.

Model: I am pretty shy, you know.

Director: Well, that's a start. You'd just have to take it to the extreme.

Model: And this will somehow cancel my looks?

Director: Yes, people will be attracted to you because of your looks nonetheless; but they will forgive you your looks because you're so shy.

Model: Tell me something. Have you done this with others before?

Director: Advised about politics? Yes, I have.

Model: Were they handsome?

Director: Very.

Model: Did you tell them to be shy?

Director: No.

Model: Why not?

Director: It wasn't in their nature. We have to work with what's in our nature, enhancing here, downplaying there.

Model: What would you downplay with me?

Director: Your looks.

Model: How?

Director: You can only wear modest clothing. Nothing very expensive. Nothing designed to show off your form.

Model: That's easy advice to follow. I don't care very much about clothes.

Director: That's one of the things that makes you unusual. Beautiful, shy, modest, thoughtful, sincere. You have a good chance of winning,

Model: Hold on. Aside from my beauty, are all these things you're describing of use to you solely to win an election?

Director: Are you asking if they're good for their own sake?

Model: Yes.

Director: Shyness isn't good for its own sake. Modesty? No, that's only good for its effect on others. Thoughtfulness—

Model: Hold on. Modesty isn't good for its own sake? Doesn't it prevent us from megalomania?

Director: Ah, you have a point. Modesty is good for that.

Model: And thoughtfulness?

Director: That can keep you out of trouble.

Model: And sincerity?

Director: It can keep you honest with yourself, which I suppose is a good thing in itself.

Model: Which of these things do you think is hardest?

Director: For you? None of them strike me as especially hard.

Model: So I'll just glide into office?

Director: Why not?

Model: Because it's not... fair!

Director: Fair to you? Sure it is. We're trying to put you in a place where you'll be more comfortable than you are now. Isn't that fair?

Model: I guess it is. We should all be put in a place where we're more comfortable than we are now. Where would you like to go?

Director: I'm comfortable now, having this conversation.

Model: But something just occurred to me. How will I be comfortable wearing modest clothing when those who give money to me will be wearing expensive clothing and they'll resent that I'm showing them up with inexpensive threads?

Director: Model, if you look for them, I'm certain you can find all kinds of discomforts in life. You'll just have to learn to ignore. That, my friend, will be what's hardest for you.

- PHILOSOPHICAL POLITICS

Model: Is it philosophical to ignore?

Director: Ignore what? Ideas? There are a lot of ideas out there. We can't take them all on at once.

Model: How do you choose an idea to take on?

Director: I try to go after the most important one at hand.

Model: So, what, some days it's justice and some days it's looks?

Director: Right, though the two can cross. For instance—is it just that you're so good looking?

Model: I don't think justice has anything to do with it.

Director: Why not?

Model: Justice is getting what you deserve. I didn't deserve these looks. I didn't not deserve them, either.

Director: Good.

Model: Good?

Director: You neatly avoided two very serious errors when it comes to these things.

Model: So what does that mean? Justice will be on my side?

Director: No, but it won't be against you, either.

Model: Why not?

Director: You don't ride rough shod over others. But you're also not the victim of your looks.

Model: Which means for me, justice has nothing to do with my looks.

Director: Yes.

Model: But you said the two can cross. And I know they can—because people think I get more breaks in this world because of my looks, and it isn't fair.

Director: Yes, but what matters is what you do with those breaks. And I like what you're doing with yours.

Model: You mean preparing for politics. But here's the thing. If I'm supposed to be so modest, how do I hide my drive to win?

Director: You have to play the reluctant candidate, whose friends persuaded him to run. And as you run, you start to believe.

Model: Believe?

Director: Believe in yourself. This has to be a sort of crescendo into the election. People will root for you, cheer you on as you grow stronger in your belief. And their belief will grow as you do.

Model: Is this philosophy?

Director: Maybe it's philosophical politics?

Model: Why not just politics?

Director: Could be. But wouldn't it be good to get a philosopher in office?

Model: Marcus Aurelius was a philosopher-emperor in Rome.

Director: Was he? I think 'philosopher' meant something different then. But the point is getting philosophy as we understand it into office.

Model: And what if when we get there we find 'philosophers' already in place?

Director: We'll philosophize with them our way and eventually drive them out.

Model: To be replaced by more philosophers like us?

Director: That's the hope.

Model: What's the end of this hope?

Director: To make a better world.

Model: By making the nation a cultivated field seeded by the wind?

Director: You sense the danger here. So I'll tell you this. There will be no shortage of planters proceeding from a plan.

Model: You're just not one of them.

Director: Right. My efforts are better spent elsewhere.

~ Swamps and Deserts

Model: Where? In breaking up the fertile soil? But what do you do when the job is done?

Director: It's a big job. But let's assume the work is done. Maybe then I'd turn to the vast stretches of county that are either desert or swamp.

Model: What would you do there?

Director: Drain the swamp; irrigate the desert. In fact, the ideal might be to drain the swamp into the desert.

Model: But what are we talking about? People's minds, right? Soggy thought; barren thought.

Director: Yes. And I think it's important to note that in each mind there is at least a little swamp and some desert.

Model: What do we do with the swamp?

Director: Tighten up our reasoning.

Model: And the desert?

Director: Loosen up a bit.

Model: It's reason to suit?

Director: We can only reason on what we're given. We have to adjust.

Model: So we should be moderate in reason?

Director: We should be immoderate in reason. We should reason all the time. But how we reason changes.

Model: But then we're giving people license to be strict or sloppy as desired?

Director: A little loose doesn't mean sloppy. Besides, we're not concerned with people who can't intuit—if only with a little help—what deserves what.

Model: What do we do? Ignore them?

Director: Yes, and seek out people who understand that there is a time to be strict and a time to be a little loose.

Model: A little loose, yes. Just enough for life.

~ BEHAVIOR

Director: Tell me something, Model.

Model: Anything.

Director: When it comes to looks, do you like to be in a swamp or a desert?

Model: When it comes to *my* looks?

Director: Sorry, no. When it comes to the looks of others.

Model: I prefer the desert, if by that we mean there are few present with good looks.

Director: So you can stand out all the more?

Model: No, not that. I just can't stand how most good looking people behave.

Director: How do they behave?

Model: Like they deserve to be in charge.

Director: Do they deserve to be in charge?

Model: Of course not. Not for that alone. And they are so lazy from their looks, they cultivate no other skills.

Director: I see. How can we change them?

Model: I don't think we can.

Director: What if we scare them?

Model: Scare them?

Director: With all the responsibilities of being in charge.

Model: That might help. But how can we scare them without putting ourselves at risk?

Director: By putting someone responsible over them.

Model: So they're in charge but only up to a point.

Director: Yes, and you might be that point—if you aim high enough, my friend.

Model: Now you've intrigued me, Director. I'd like to rule over the good looking. Does that surprise you?

Director: A little. How would you behave toward them?

Model: It would depend on how they behave toward me.

Director: If they look up to you?

Model: I'd make a wonderful friend.

Director: And if they resented you, were jealous of you—if they sought to cut you down to size?

Model: Since I've already cut myself down to size, I wouldn't appreciate their efforts.

Director: What would you do?

Model: I would crush these ants with force.

Director: Hold on. What force would you use?

Model: A withering look.

Director: Okay. Phew! I was a little worried there.

Model: What were you worried about?

Director: Tyranny.

Model: Director.

Director: Sorry, but someone with your gifts is always at risk of becoming tyrannical.

Model: Tyrannical in office or tyrannical in love?

Director: Good question. Both.

Model: Why do the good looking become tyrannical?

Director: They're used to getting what they want.

Model: That's it?

Director: That's much. How many people don't get what they want?

Model: All those who want too much.

Director: Who's to say how much is too much?

Model: I'm to say.

Director: You're sure about that?

Model: I know the human heart well. The hearts that want too much turn black.

Director: Are you talking about oversized ambition?

Model: I am. And it turns evil in the end.

- TAILORS, CLIMBING

Director: Maybe that's what philosophers are.

Model: What? Evil?

Director: No, tailors. They help tailor ambition to suit.

Model: Preventing evil, yes. They know what fits a particular soul. But, Director, philosophers as philosophers have no power at their disposal. How can they effect what they know?

Director: They simply show the ambitious what a good fit is like. And then they let them take it from there.

Model: But even if the size of the ambition is right, there is a fight. A fight to gain position or place; a fight to maintain position or place.

Director: There's always a fight. Even if you want to climb down, they'll fight you to the bottom.

Model: They should let you down if you want down.

Director: But then you're an insult to their aspirations.

Model: So there must be something wrong for you to want down.

Director: Yes. It can't just be that you wanted down.

Model: But some people have every opportunity in the world, and they turn them all down.

Director: Why do you think they do?

Model: They don't like what they see.

Director: Maybe they didn't like what they saw because they weren't fit.

Model: Fit for something they don't like? I'd say that's good! But do they really have to go all the way to the bottom?

Director: Some of them do. It makes for a sort of symmetry in their life. From the highest high to the lowest low. There might be an odd satisfaction here.

Model: I think it's better to maintain your level all throughout life—not too high, not too low.

Director: There's something to what you say. But curiosity sometimes gets the better of us.

Model: You think some people climb out of simple curiosity?

Director: I do.

Model: Why didn't you?

Director: How do you know I didn't?

Model: Did you?

Director: I've done my share of climbing in life.

Model: But you never came down?

Director: Why do you say that?

Model: You're a director in a corporation.

Director: There are much higher positions in life. Mine is a middling height that gives me something of a view.

Model: You like this view?

Director: I can see the up and comers from here. Surely that's not bad.

Model: And you intercept them, and try to be a tailor to them.

Director: I try to be a philosopher to them. I want to purge their bad beliefs come what may.

Model: What may come?

Director: I prefer to leave that to chance.

- LIMITED

Model: You leave it to chance so there's no blame on you!

Director: I leave it to chance because that's how these things work.

Model: You can't suggest a good belief?

Director: I can't.

Model: Why not?

Director: I don't know what's good for others.

Model: But you know what's bad?

Director: Yes.

Model: You're rather limited in your view.

Director: Indeed I am. But at least I don't pretend otherwise.

Model: Does this go for all things? I mean, if I ask you what is the square root of 222, you might not know the answer; but if I say it's 7, you can tell me I'm wrong.

Director: Yes, I'll be sure to tell you it's wrong.

Model: So you, as a philosopher, don't know what's right—you only know what's wrong.

Director: And I'm very valuable in that way.

Model: If I were in office, I'd like for you to advise me. You'd let me decide what's right, if it weren't clearly wrong.

Director: That's what I can do for you, yes.

Model: You'd give me free rein, within limits.

Director: And within those limits I'd trust you to find open and hopeful chance.

Model: The electorate must trust me in this.

Director: You're really tempted to run?

Model: I really am. I just think there's a lot of risk.

Director: But think of the benefit—being where you belong. And if we're wrong about this, you can always step down.

Model: And down and down.

Director: Yes, but don't be afraid. There's a wonderful prize... when you bottom.

- Bottom

Model: What prize, Director?

Director: Freedom.

Model: Don't tell me that.

Director: Why not?

Model: Because it's pathetic. And it's a lie.

Director: How so?

Model: Even at the bottom, lower is possible still.

Director: Still?

Model: We can always sink lower. Even earning minimum wage is higher than it is for some. And there's pressure here, too.

Director: What pressure?

Model: Those down from the heights will, if only out of habit, seek to rise.

Director: So if they end up working in the crew, they'll want to rise to crew chief?

Model: Yes, even if the move amounts to only a dollar more.

Director: Only a dollar? Then why?

Model: Because it involves more authority—and promise of things to come.

Director: Do you think a philosopher would care about a dollar and promise of things to come?

Model: You tell me.

Director: I'm sure the dollar would come in handy. But promise? Promotion? To what end? And at what price?

Model: What's the price typically paid?

Director: Responsibility.

Model: And what does that mean?

Director: You own what happens.

Model: Do you like to own what happens?

Director: I don't much care to be responsible for others, if that's what you mean.

Model: But you are responsible for others at work. So what do you do?

Director: I choose good people to work with.

Model: And if you were responsible for others not of your choice?

Director: I'd say it's not fair.

Model: Ha! Well, I think it's true. But how do you know who to choose?

Director: It often helps if they've touched bottom.

Model: Why does that matter?

Director: Because they likely don't want to do it again.

Model: Would you hire me?

Director: No.

Model: Why not? I haven't sunk low enough for you?

Director: You're destined for greater things.

Model: Who do you hire, bottom aside?

Director: Allies of philosophy.

Model: To help you win what fight?

Director: The only fight philosophy ever fights. The fight against false belief.

~ FALSE BELIEF

Model: Yes, this is what you say. But what about true belief?

Director: What about it?

Model: Do you fight that?

Director: How would I fight it?

Model: You might say belief, true or false, is only belief. Knowledge, however, is what we're after. Knowledge is always true.

Director: But isn't true belief always true?

Model: Do you think it is?

Director: If it weren't, why would we call it true?

Model: Let's have an example.

Director: I believe gorillas are strong. Is that a true belief?

Model: Sure, but you could know gorillas are strong.

Director: What's the difference?

Model: To believe, you might have read about their strength. To know, you might have encountered some in the wild.

Director: That's an excellent point. Belief is at a remove; knowledge is at first hand.

Model: I think that holds up. You can never know until you know; but you can believe whenever you like.

Director: Maybe that's all philosophy does.

Model: What do you mean?

Director: It says you should chase down every belief and replace it with first-hand knowledge.

Model: But people believe a great many things. Maybe they only have time to chase down the most important ones.

Director: Then they should chase down whatever important beliefs they can. And we can help them here.

Model: How?

Director: We can tell them which beliefs are truly important and worth chasing down.

Model: How do we do that?

Director: Through dialogue, of course. We look for what they strongly believe, so strongly that our words have no effect.

Model: But if our words have no effect, how can we persuade them to chase down their belief?

Director: We have to tantalize them. Make this seem like the most at-tractive thing in the world.

Model: How do we do that?

Director: We reason with them.

Model: And if they're not open to reason?

Director: We've picked the wrong one to talk to, my friend.

Model: Is it the right one to talk to if they're open to reason but riddled with false belief?

Director: Yes, but we have to be careful.

Model: Why?

Director: They might suspect what we're about and become defensive.

Model: Meaning they close themselves to reason.

Director: They sometimes do.

Model: And they do this because they suspect their beliefs are false.

Director: That's often the case.

Model: But no one can know a belief is false until it's proven false.

Director: So you see we have to allay their fears and get them to talk.

Model: How?

Director: I don't know.

Model: What do you mean? How can you proceed without knowing?

Director: It isn't easy. I just stay ready for the slightest break in the fear.

Model: And that's all it takes?

Director: That's much.

Model: But what if there's no break?

Director: We just stay ready, nonetheless.

- UGLY

Model: But we can't stay forever ready.

Director: Why not?

Model: It's exhausting!

Director: You get used to it.

Model: But what if their fear becomes explosive?

Director: I've learned not to let things blow up in my face.

Model: What's the secret?

Director: Being a good judge of character.

Model: How do you judge?

Director: By how open they are to philosophy when they're not afraid.

Model: You know, no one else judges that way.

Director: Then it's a good thing I'm not no one else. But there's more to it than that. I have to judge how quickly and over what they become afraid.

Model: How quickly and over what do I become afraid?

Director: You very quickly become afraid of your own shadow.

Model: Ha!

Director: But it's true! Your shadow is as beautiful as you are. And, for some reason, you're afraid of that beauty.

Model: And yet you find me beautiful?

Director: I do. But you'd be even more beautiful if you got rid of this fear.

Model: Because my soul would grow more beautiful.

Director: Yes. It would match the beauty of your body.

Model: Is matching the ideal? I mean, suppose someone has an ugly body; should the soul be ugly, too?

Director: Should it? Of course not.

Model: Would you say someone with a beautiful soul but wretchedly ugly body is beautiful?

Director: Without a doubt.

Model: You're just saying that because it sounds good.

Director: You don't think I'd be attracted to them?

Model: To someone that ugly? Of course you wouldn't.

Director: You're wrong.

Model: Then let me blunt. Have you ever slept with someone brutally ugly who has a good personality, as they say?

Director: I have.

Model: You're honestly that attracted to soul?

Director: I am.

Model: You're going to have to forgive me again if I speak what's on my mind.

Director: Please do. I expect nothing less.

Model: Maybe you only slept with them because you couldn't do better. I'm sorry, but I had to say it.

Director: No apology necessary. It's a natural question. But I have proof. I've slept with those who have conventionally beautiful looks. And it was better with what you would call ugly. I can supply you with references if you'd like.

Model: No, I believe you. But I must admit, I'm a little in shock. I thought I knew the truth. But in believing you, I must admit I'm wrong.

Director: This is one of the things I admire about you. You accept the facts. But what about you?

Model: What about me?

Director: Why haven't you slept with soul instead of looks?

Model: I felt the power relationship was off.

Director: Too one sided in your looks?

Model: Yes. And I didn't feel they cared for me for what I really am.

Director: The ugly wanted you for your beautiful looks. They didn't care about your soul.

Model: Yes, and I couldn't stomach that.

Director: That's to your credit, I think.

Model: Why do you only 'think'?

Director: Because I suspect there's more to the story.

~ JUSTICE TO THE THING

Model: What more could there be?

Director: Tell me, and be honest now. Did you think these ugly people were beneath you?

Model: I felt I'd be taking advantage of them.

Director: What advantage? They wanted to sleep with you. You wanted to sleep with them. Or didn't you?

Model: I didn't.

Director: Why not?

Model: They were... ugly!

Director: They weren't attractive to you.

Model: Exactly. You can't help who you're attracted to, Director.

Director: Yes, but you can lie to yourself about who you are.

Model: Who you are, or who you're attracted to?

Director: What's the difference?

Model: That's a good point. I think we're defined by our attractions. Don't you?

Director: I might change my mind, but right now that's what I think.

Model: And you're really attracted to character.

Director: I really am.

Model: What sort of character?

Director: Oh, it's a *je ne sais quoi*. I just don't know.

Model: Well, for you to resort to another language says much! But try, Director, try to explain.

Director: There has to be a spark, a liveliness, a loveliness. Something daring.

Model: Daring against what?

Director: Everything. The world. Society. Oppression. Pain. Suffering. Injustice. Justice. You name it.

Model: Hold on. Now I think you're telling me a story. How can you dare to be against both justice and injustice at once?

Director: Because sometimes justice is 'justice' and injustice is 'injustice'. I want someone who can dare to walk away from all that.

Model: So, to be clear, you want someone who doesn't care about justice, whatever it means.

Director: Yes. But they have to be deeply passionate about it at the same time.

Model: You're impossible. You want someone with a passion for justice who doesn't care about justice? How?

Director: What is justice?

Model: As I've said. Getting what you deserve.

Director: The passion-for-justice I want has to do with words. Description. Praise and blame.

Model: You love people who tell it like it is, who do justice to the thing.

Director: Yes, even when it comes to myself. In fact, I find that most attractive of all.

Model: Because you put on no airs. You want people who tell it like it is because you come out well. And look at you grin!

Director: How about you? Would you come out well?

Model: I don't know.

Director: How can you not know? Don't you know yourself?

Model: Too many people tell me stories about who I am in order to manipulate me. How can I possibly know myself that well?

Director: I think your fight is harder than mine.

Model: Thank you, I think.

Director: But, Model? That's no excuse.

- EXCUSES

Model: I know what you mean. Boo hoo, poor me. So many people want to puff me up or cut me down, I don't know which end is up.

Director: Yes, but I think someone like me can have it hard as well. Many people want to cut me down. But I get used to it. And then along comes someone else, someone who puffs me up. Isn't the risk that I'd be a sucker for it?

Model: I take your point. And I think it's true. Especially if it's someone like me, someone with exceptionally beautiful looks. Not that I'm saying you're not handsome in your way, but you know what I mean.

Director: Strictly by looks I'm average, yes. But I like to think my character is as exceptionally beautiful as are your physical looks.

Model: Then I'll tell you in all honesty. Your character is the best looking thing I've seen.

Director: But your character is beautiful, too, though it could stand some improvement. I'd like to see you become more beautiful than I am.

Model: Why? Don't you feel rivalry?

Director: I want to improve. And if you become more beautiful, I will have someone to look to as I try to improve.

Model: Surely you have others you admire.

Director: Oh, I do—in bits and pieces. But I'm looking for the whole, the whole that's so rare. You might be the one to achieve it.

Model: Tell me about this whole.

Director: Well, it requires that you make no excuses for yourself. And it takes a total inner honesty.

Model: No easy things.

Director: No, not easy. But here's the hardest part. If you encounter someone with a similar honesty, you have to speak truth to them.

Model: That doesn't sound so hard.

Director: We're talking about the whole truth and nothing but the truth.

Model: Well, that's a different story. But, Director, it's always seemed to me that we need to keep something for ourselves.

Director: Maybe that's what's holding you back.

Model: Do you share everything?

Director: I haven't met the right person yet. But, I can say this—I've shared all of me around in different places; some things here, some things there.

Model: I guess that's a sort of second best.

Director: Yes, but I want the best. Don't you?

Model: Sure. But here's the thing. You might be my 'best'. I might be able to share everything with you. But if you don't reciprocate? What if I'm not your best? Do you know what I mean?

Director: I was thinking just the same about you!

Model: You're flattering me.

Director: No. And I'll tell you why. Your good looks, your all but perfect looks, make you strong in some ways. You have a kind of confidence that makes you stand tall. This confidence, this knowledge of things and how they work, might make you able to withstand my truth without blinking. Do you know what I mean?

Model: I think I know exactly what you mean. So try me. What's the truth about you? No flinching, and no excuses now, Director.

Director: The truth about philosophy is the truth about me.

Model: What's that supposed to mean?

Director: If you want to know about me, you have to know about philosophy.

Model: You're both constructive and destructive at once?

Director: No, not at once. It doesn't work that way.

Model: But you want to build me up into my full character.

Director: I want you to be what you can be.

Model: And you know what? I'm grateful for that.

- The Irony

Director: But I want you to understand philosophy so you can understand me.

Model: Here's the thing. I think you'll say you have to live philosophy in order to understand it. So you're just saying 'you have to walk a mile in my shoes before you can know who I am'.

Director: Do you think it's the same with you?

Model: Yes, I do. You can 'know' what it means to be beautiful. But unless you feel what it means, feel it yourself in my shoes—you really can't know.

Director: So we're all just islands in the stream?

Model: I'm afraid so.

Director: Then my friend the writer was right.

Model: What do you mean?

Director: He spends his life writing about what it means to be him.

Model: Do you understand him any the better for it?

Director: I'm not sure—and he knows it.

Model: Is his writing a waste of time?

Director: No more than any human endeavor.

Model: All is folly?

Director: Except for good looks.

Model: I know you don't mean it. Character is what counts.

Director: The character that suits the body, yes.

Model: I'd be grateful if you could explain what that means.

Director: There's an old way of thinking that says each type of body has a character that suits it well. Figure it out for yourself, and happiness is yours.

Model: Happiness? Really?

Director: Well, maybe not happiness. But satisfaction.

Model: I'd take satisfaction over happiness, and be grateful for it.

Director: Why?

Model: Because happiness is on the surface, and can be blown away by the wind. Satisfaction is deep, and hard to dislodge.

Director: Interesting. You're persuading me to choose satisfaction, too.

Model: So what does it mean for you? You have the body of a philosopher? I don't think you can say that seriously.

Director: No, I can't. Philosophers can come in all shapes and sizes. But, that said, there are different kinds of philosophers.

Model: And that's determined by their shape?

Director: Yes. And I think it will be heartening to you to learn that some philosophers' shapes are so unusual that they aren't even generally recognized as philosophers.

Model: What are they, undercover philosophers?

Director: Yes, just so. You might be one.

Model: But philosophers speak and give themselves away. How could I remain undercover?

Director: You'll speak in all seriousness, but people will think you're kidding, or being sarcastic. They won't accept that you are what you are.

Model: What kind of life is that?

Director: One you might enjoy.

Model: How?

Director: You have to revel in the irony.

Model: You know, people always talk about irony. But I don't know what it is.

Director: The classical meaning of irony involves dissembling what you know.

Model: You pretend to be dumb?

Director: That's what Socrates did.

Model: I could do that! And people would believe it!

Director: Then I think you're on your way.

~ THE WAY

Model: Irony for me would be easy. People just assume I'm dumb.

Director: I won't deny you have an advantage here. But can you explain why it's good to play dumb?

Model: You can get people to say things they wouldn't otherwise say. And you can say things you couldn't otherwise say.

Director: I think that's a very good insight. My friend the writer plays dumb. His style is simple. He doesn't use big words. He describes most things in a naive way. And then he lets slip the truth.

Model: I want to read your friend.

Director: I'll ask him to send you one of his books. But tell me, Model, what do you hope to learn from him?

Model: Learn? I just want to enjoy!

Director: Ha! A good reason indeed. I think you're on your way.

Model: But you're right. I do need to learn. I want to perfect my character.

Director: Some people think character is an act.

Model: Well, everything we do is a sort of act. So, sure, character is an act. It's what we habitually do.

Director: But sometimes we don't do what we habitually do. I think these times are important. What do you think?

Model: Character is never perfect. Or, let me rephrase. Character should never be perfect.

Director: Why not?

Model: Because it's suffocating when it is.

Director: So if we have good character we should sometimes be bad?

Model: No, it's not so much that. We have to be willing to question what our character is. We have to assume it's not perfect. But while questioning we have to stay true, yet make adjustments when we know what must change.

Director: Change and stay true at once? A difficult thing.

Model: Of course. That's the way.

Director: How can we tell if another's character is true?

Model: Through dialogue—and watching what they do.

Director: You've expressed a desire to be a philosopher. Is it so you can know what's true?

Model: There's nothing more I want to know.

Director: Does it really take being a philosopher to know what's true?

Model: In one sense, of course not. The world would stop turning if people didn't know what's true.

Director: Sometimes I get dizzy from all the turning. And sometimes I think people only know what's 'true'.

Model: Tell me what is 'true'.

Director: Mostly? It's comfort. Comfort is 'true'—and maybe without the quotes.

Model: Creature comfort?

Director: Yes. But then there are those who project their comfort out across the years.

Model: The prudent.

Director: Right. Delayed gratification as the hallmark of civilization.

Model: Do you think it *is* the hallmark of civilization?

Director: For the most part? Yes.

Model: Then you'd better explain.

~ CIVILIZATION

Director: It comes down to this. Is comfort good?

Model: Of course. But there are things that are better.

Director: Agreed. What are those things?

Model: Love, true love.

Director: True love can be uncomfortable?

Model: Yes, of course.

Director: I think many people would shy away from love because of that.

Model: They want comfortable marriages and the like.

Director: Are comfortable marriages the bedrock of civilization?

Model: They say the family is that.

Director: And what's a good family based upon?

Model: Comfortable marriages.

Director: Everything follows from that?

Model: Yes, everything follows from that.

Director: So comfort is king. And don't be shy to admit this truth, if it's a truth.

Model: I think for most it's the truth.

Director: So there's virtue in comfort?

Model: Yes. Or should I say 'virtue'?

Director: You can say what you like, but I think there's virtue in it. After all, how do you weather the storms of life without this bedrock comfort?

Model: You make a good point.

Director: So, next time, be careful when you choose to put words like 'virtue' in quotes.

Model: I will.

Director: Now, we have to ask if civilization is good.

Model: Of course it's good! What would you have us be? Barbarians?

Director: Do you know where the word 'barbarian' comes from?

Model: No, I don't.

Director: It's from the Ancient Greek. When they heard people speaking foreign tongues, they said it sounded like 'bar bar bar'. So they called them barbarians.

Model: Barbarian just meant people who didn't speak Greek?

Director: Yes.

Model: The Greeks were xenophobes?

Director: Of course they were.

Model: And here we are holding them up as examples of I don't know what!

Director: Yes, and they held slaves and gave women few rights.

Model: Why does this never come up?

Director: It does come up, but not where you usually listen.

Model: But some people hold them up as the height of civilization.

Director: Some people hold us up as the height of civilization.

Model: Do you think we are?

Director: It depends what we mean by civilization.

Model: Now you're just taking the easy way out.

Director: Okay. No, I don't think we're the height of civilization.

Model: What is the height?

Director: Oh, I don't know. Pick your poison. Byzantine Constantinople? Florentine Italy? Sun King France? Britain's Empire? And those are only the ones I've studied. China might have a claim. Persia. Egypt. And so on.

Model: What do they all have in common?

Director: A certain disposition toward families, ruling class or not.

~ FAMILIES

Model: But all societies have 'a certain disposition toward families'.

Director: That goes to show just how important families are. But tell me something, Model. How many models go on to have a strong family life? Is it in keeping with the general population trend? Or is it more or less?

Model: I've never given it much thought. But I'm inclined to say it's less.

Director: Why do you think that is?

Model: Many models are selfish.

Director: And selfish people don't form strong family bonds?

Model: I think that's true, don't you?

Director: I think it's the opposite.

Model: How so?

Director: People want families for selfish reasons. They want the comfort, yes. But they also want emotional and other support. And they want a legacy.

Model: They want immortality.

Director: Sure. Do you doubt any of this?

Model: No, I think it's spot on.

Director: So what about your models? What do they want?

Model: I... don't know. I mean, they want shallow things. Fame, money, and so on. Those are selfish things.

Director: Is it safe to say everyone wants selfish things?

Model: Yes.

Director: So there's nothing wrong with being selfish. Or will you say there's 'selfish' and then there's selfish?

Model: No, selfish is selfish. It's just that some things build beyond themselves.

Director: Some things like families.

Model: Yes.

Director: Are you sure models, many of them at least, don't build beyond themselves?

Model: I'm sure of it, yes. But are we saying families are simply good?

Director: I'm not sure anything is simply good.

Model: But each civilization has its simply good. And in many of them family is simply good.

Director: And with them, to be outside the family is bad.

Model: Of course.

Director: What's the distinctive feature of our civilization?

Model: Family is king.

Director: But?

Model: There are exceptions.

Director: So it's not simply bad to be outside the family.

Model: No, it's not.

Director: You have no family to speak of. And you just might get elected to office.

Model: It's true.

Director: So family is king except when it's not.

Model: But even then people expect you to pay obeisance every time you speak.

Director: The king will have his due.

Model: The king should be more broad minded than that.

Director: Is a broad minded king good for civilization?

Model: A broad minded king should be the end of civilization.

– FIRST, NOBLE

Director: I agree. But I'm particular in how I judge.

Model: What do you mean?

Director: I rank civilizations based on how open they are to philosophy.

Model: Of course you do. How does ours stand?

Director: I'm still alive and working away.

Model: You don't have a very high standard, do you?

Director: It doesn't take much.

Model: Can I have office and have philosophy, too?

Director: Philosophy is a jealous mistress. So it won't be easy on you.

Model: Philosophy isn't a wife?

Director: Ah, metaphors. What can I say? Socrates was married.

Model: Sure, but what other philosophers were?

Director: Machiavelli, if you count him as a philosopher.

Model: Who else?

Director: Strauss. But what's the point, Model? Some philosophers marry; some don't.

Model: Yes, but the truth is that philosophy comes first.

Director: That's like saying yourself comes first.

Model: Well, that's the point, now, isn't it? Families involve putting the other family members first.

Director: I'm not sure there's anything that involves putting other people first.

Model: I can just hear countless mothers telling you that they put their children first.

Director: What do models put first?

Model: For as long as they can? Their careers. Many of them, at least.

Director: And that's the thing. We can only speak in generalities about these things. If we want to get specific we need a particular example.

Model: I'm a particular example.

Director: So you are. What do you want?

Model: I... don't know.

Director: Career? Family? Money?

Model: None of it really interests me. That's why I think philosophy might be it.

Director: What is philosophy? Some sort of last resort?

Model: No! Like I said, I think it's noble.

Director: So you want the noble.

Model: Yes.

Director: You're better off in politics.

Model: How can you say that? I thought you wanted to win people to the cause.

Director: I want to win over those who belong to the cause. The more I think about it, the more I think you belong in politics.

Model: For selfish reasons?

Director: Whose selfish reasons? Yours or mine? I want you in politics for selfish reasons—I want to be well led. You want politics for selfish reasons—you want nobility, however much is possible here.

Model: Why do you think we can't have political nobility here?

Director: Don't get me wrong. I think we can have wonderful things in politics. Things to be admired. But nobility, in the old sense of the word? Impossible.

Model: But that's not what I'm after. I want nobility in the new sense of the word.

Director: What's noble in our land?

Model: Our tolerance of other points of view.

Director: The old nobility was markedly intolerant.

Model: Not all of them. They're the ones who helped bring about the new meaning of 'noble'.

Director: Since you know that, you must also know that the new tolerance was considered by many to be a form of corruption.

Model: That's no surprise. Progress and 'corruption' often go hand in hand.

~ CORRUPTION, DISTRIBUTION OF THE BEAUTIFUL

Director: Corruption in morals?

Model: Is there another kind of corruption?

Director: No, I think morals is it. But do you think the new corruption always wins out against the old nobility?

Model: Doesn't it?

Director: It's anyone's guess. History is littered with different endings. But usually when there's such a battle, the nation is destined to do one of two things. Fall, or reinvent itself.

Model: It's true. Nations aren't stagnant things. They evolve. But sometimes they change, just like that.

Director: Or so it seems. I think there are signs. And I think the good looking play a part.

Model: How? I've never heard a theory like this before.

Director: To call it a theory is too much. I just think the distribution of the beautiful in a society has a great effect.

Model: What distribution causes what?

Director: Well, I think a natural distribution—the beautiful stay where the beautiful were born—helps keep the fabric of society intact. But when the beautiful concentrate, usually in the capital, I think there's trouble in store.

Model: Why?

Director: It's very hard to say. All I can say for now is that it has an effect on human values.

Model: Let me guess. It creates a marketplace for beauty.

Director: Yes, and the effects are profound.

Model: You don't have to tell me. Everyone looks to the capital for more than what they should. So you're opposed to the concentration of beauty?

Director: I love beauty. I would see it concentrated if I could. But I love the beauty of soul. To concentrate that is like herding cats.

Model: I don't see why. I think a city full of 'cats' would be someplace you'd love to be; and it would provide good examples for those in the provinces to see.

Director: Would you like to be one? To be a role model?

Model: Honestly? I would.

Director: Then let it be politics for you.

Model: I'm tempted.

Director: Then take the first step.

Model: But what about philosophy?

Director: I think you can make more impact as a politician than as a philosopher.

Model: Why more impact as a politician?

Director: I, as a philosopher, usually talk to one person at a time. You, as a politician, will talk to millions if things go well. And if they don't go that well, you'll still be talking to thousands.

Model: But that's only tempting if I have something to say.

- TEMPTATION, PRESENTATION, NATURAL FIT

Director: I have my own temptation along these lines.

Model: Oh? What is it?

Director: To say too much or too little.

Model: What's wrong with saying too much?

Director: I scare people off.

Model: And too little?

Director: I don't intrigue them enough.

Model: You're talking about scaring them off from philosophy, intriguing them toward philosophy.

Director: Yes, it's a delicate matter.

Model: Why do you think that is?

Director: Because philosophy, too, has looks, has appearance.

Model: So one person might have a good looking philosophy and another an ugly one?

Director: Yes, that's true.

Model: But it's not a matter of too many or not enough words. It has to do with how you present the truth about philosophy, what philosophy is.

Director: Well, you're right. If your presentation doesn't have some beauty to it, you can forget the whole thing.

Model: The beauty of your philosophy is a sort of temptation to your listener, isn't it?

Director: Yes, I'm tempting them to engage in philosophy. Ultimately, I'm tempting them to become philosophers.

Model: So you don't do the ultimate with me. You want me to be a politician.

Director: You're the one who has to want what you'll be. If you want philosophy, I'd be glad.

Model: You mean if I really want it. If I'm meant to be a philosopher.

Director: Yes, it has to be a natural fit.

Model: But you can tell if it's a natural fit, can't you?

Director: I've been surprised before, but for the most part—yes.

Model: Why would philosophy ever be a temptation? I mean, we don't say I'm tempted to become a salesperson; we don't say I'm tempted to become a doctor.

Director: Philosophy is tempting because it's generally frowned upon and involves a significant degree of danger.

Model: Why is it frowned upon?

Director: People tend to frown when you question their cherished beliefs.

Model: Why is it dangerous?

Director: People can react very strongly to questioning of their cherished beliefs.

Model: I can see that.

Director: Do you think you're up for it?

Model: I'd rather stand up and speak political words, words of belief.

Director: Even though you're a bit shy?

Model: It's easier to speak like that than to challenge.

Director: Won't your speeches be challenging?

Model: They'll seek to push the boundaries of the possible, yes. But they won't tell the voters they're out-and-out wrong.

~ Don't Believe, Believe

Model: But now I want to talk about philosopher-kings, like that Roman emperor.

Director: Well, a philosopher-king must tell the people when they're wrong. 'Don't believe what you believe about this. Don't believe what you believe about that.'

Model: Yes, but then you say, 'But believe in this! Believe in that!'

Director: Let's talk about what's possible for a Congressperson in the United States today. What happens if you say, 'Don't believe in this'?

Model: It depends on the belief. I might say don't believe in the other party, and that would be fine.

Director: What about this? 'Don't believe in the justice of this country toward other nations.'

Model: There is a crowd that would play to well. But I'm not sure it's the majority.

Director: Then what about this? 'People shouldn't have the right to vote because they're by and large ignorant about affairs.'

Model: First of all, I don't think that's true. People know a lot more than we might think. Secondly, even if it were true, there's something wrong about telling your voters not to vote.

Director: What if you tell them, 'Don't believe in God'?

Model: That would get me booed off the stage in most places.

Director: What if you tell them to stop believing in the family because it does more harm than good?

Model: Director, are you trying to get me killed?

Director: I'm just fishing around to see what you think.

Model: Yes, but you know what I think on all these things.

Director: You think like a democratic politician, not some autocrat. At one point or another autocrats have attempted just about every kind of forced unbelief.

Model: And that makes you nervous.

Director: Why do you think that?

Model: Because they're acting like philosophers.

Director: Philosophers don't force anything.

Model: But they're aiming at the same ends.

Director: Are they? There's an important difference here. Philosophers might fish around from time to time to see what's to be seen. But they don't expect obedience.

Model: True.

Director: And the first thing a tyrant would say to a philosopher is, 'Oh, just shut up!'

Model: Because a philosopher would ask, 'Do you really think people will be happier without God, without families, without everything they believe in?'

Director: The tyrant might say, 'I don't care if they're happy or not. I won't have false belief in my land. Let the chips fall where they may.'

Model: But believing in the family isn't a false belief. Bad families are bad because the people in them don't believe enough!

Director: Here's something I wonder. If you believe in something, do you, of some sort of necessity, act in accordance with your belief?

Model: Yes. Belief, true belief, makes us act.

Director: Can we tell by the acts if a person has the belief?

Model: Over time? Yes, we can.

Director: So a good politician, or a tyrant even, could sit back and watch what people do and be able to determine what they believe?

Model: Yes, a skilled politician or autocrat, sure.

Director: Then what's the good of philosophy?

- PHILOSOPHY, MOTIVE

Model: I don't understand.

Director: Philosophy asks questions in order to see what people think. If a philosopher can tell what people think by watching what they do, what's the point of asking questions?

Model: You want to get *them* to see what they think.

Director: People don't know what they think?

Model: You'd be surprised. People often do things because they assume that's what's to be done. No thinking involved.

Director: Okay. We need to show them what they think, or don't. But we also need to learn what they think ourselves.

Model: I thought we were going to watch what they do.

Director: We are. But we can't take the chance.

Model: What do you mean? What chance?

Director: That we might be misled.

Model: Can you give an example?

Director: A man gets up every morning and gets out a rug and kneels on it then bows all the way to the ground. He does this a number of times then gets up and goes about his business. What does he think?

Model: He thinks he's praying to his god.

Director: So we ask him what he thinks he's doing, and he says, 'I have a bad back; I stretch it every day.'

Model: So things can appear to be other than they are. It has to do with motives.

Director: Yes. The thing is still the thing. The question is one of motive. Consider this. I never missed a class in college. People thought it was because I was incredibly devoted to learning. But really, I just loved to ask the other students questions after class about what the professor said. Do you have anything like this in your life?

Model: Hold on. Didn't you ever ask the professors questions about what they said?

Director: I should have told you. I never missed a professor's office hours in four years.

Model: You kept on going back? Why? Were you trying to impress them so you'd get a good grade?

Director: No. In fact, I think my grades suffered.

Model: Why?

Director: Because the professors thought I was thick headed.

Model: What would make them think that?

Director: I kept on asking the same questions from different angles, hoping I'd understand their replies.

Model: Sometimes I'm like that with people on a shoot, at times when we're just waiting around. People say things and I often don't understand what they mean. So I ask.

Director: How do they react?

Model: They think I'm teasing them, or being sarcastic, or whatever.

Director: Why do they think that?

Model: Because they believe I must surely know what they're talking about and I'm just trying to cause trouble.

Director: So it's a question of motive.

Model: Yes.

Director: Do they answer you eventually?

Model: I usually give up before they do. Not very philosophical of me, is it?

Director: No, it's not. But for a politician, that's not too bad.

\- Sarcasm, Strength

Director: Why was it hard to understand what your colleagues were saying?

Model: Because a lot of what they say is sarcastic.

Director: These are the good looking people being this way?

Model: Yes.

Director: Do the ugly ones around the set do the same?

Model: There aren't many ugly ones around the set.

Director: But the ones who are there, are they sarcastic?

Model: They often lead the sarcastic choir.

Director: What is sarcasm?

Model: It's a kind of mockery that shows contempt.

Director: That doesn't sound very healthy.

Model: I despise sarcasm.

Director: Why?

Model: Because it's weak, it stems from weakness.

Director: So you despise weakness?

Model: I... never thought about it that way before. That doesn't sound good.

Director: The question is whether it's true.

Model: Well, all of us have strength we can tap into. And if we don't....

Director: All of us have strength? Is this another democratic platitude I'm about to hear?

Model: You don't think we all have strength somewhere inside?

Director: This is like going to a tidal pool and saying, 'Look, you have water inside—just like the ocean, here.'

Model: I don't despise the weak.

Director: Okay. But what are the weak like?

Model: They can't stand up straight and tall. They speak sarcasm. They run down others behind their backs.

Director: And some of them are quite beautiful to look at.

Model: Yes.

Director: If they weren't beautiful, would you despise them less?

Model: I would.

Director: Why?

Model: Because the beautiful have every advantage in this world.

Director: Apparently they have only one advantage—and they know it. I think they're often sick.

Model: How so?

Director: People project great expectations onto them because of their wonderful looks. But the inner strength doesn't always match the outer form.

Model: They're hollow inside.

Director: Sure. But you, Model, you're not hollow inside. Why do you think that is?

Model: I don't know. I've always thought about things.

Director: But surely the others have thought about things, too. Don't we all think?

Model: No, we don't all think. Thinking is hard.

Director: Then what do these people do?

Model: They play with ideas.

Director: Play with ideas? What does that mean?

Model: They toy with notions then bounce them off others sarcastically. So it would seem they've thought about much but they haven't.

Director: Do they call this worldliness, sophistication?

Model: That's exactly what they call it. And part of this involves not taking anything seriously.

Director: And you think this is a reaction to things that are projected on them thanks to their beauty of form.

Model: Yes, they feel pressure from the projections—and they can't take the pressure. So they attack its source, and everything else while they're at it.

- GOOD FROM GOOD, ACTING

Director: Can you say more about the source of the pressure they feel?

Model: It comes from a belief. Good must come from good.

Director: For instance, good character comes from good looks.

Model: Right. It sounds ridiculous when you say it aloud. But this is how people think.

Director: And good thoughts come from good character?

Model: This is the next belief, yes.

Director: But your colleagues know this isn't true.

Model: Of course. Good thoughts, deeds, whatever—these things are hard. So when someone assumes you have these things because of how you look, a certain bitterness forms in your mouth.

Director: And out of the mouth spews sarcasm. Why?

Model: Because you want their good opinion of you; and you don't want their good opinion of you.

Director: You want to be known as good but you also want the truth.

Model: Right. And it's infinitely easier to be sarcastic than it is to live up to your good looks.

Director: Or to confess the truth and disappoint your audience.

Model: Audience, yes. That's the thing. We all live as if we were actors on stage.

Director: And we shouldn't?

Model: That's the worst thing we can do. Life is no act.

Director: But people applaud when we do well, and boo or hiss when we don't.

Model: I don't care. You have to live with nothing in reserve.

Director: What does that mean?

Model: Actors, when they act, know they're only acting—that they're really someone else. That's their reserve. This is a very dangerous way of thinking when it comes to real life. 'Oh, I'll only act this way for a while; I know I'm someone else.' The problem is, if you act a certain way, you become that way.

Director: Because of habit?

Model: Yes, habit; and because life is what we do.

Director: And the beautiful people don't have to do.

Model: But that's the thing. Of course they have to do. That's the biggest lie there is, that they have to do nothing.

Director: Is there anyone who has to do nothing? Philosophers, perhaps?

Model: Philosophers question and discuss. That's something.

Director: Anyone can question and discuss.

Model: Yes, but philosophers are in earnest. They really want to know.

Director: So do many who question and discuss. How do philosophers differ from them?

Model: Philosophers are ironic.

Director: Do you mean sarcastic?

Model: No, ironic. Socrates was ironic. He pretended to be dumb.

Director: Why do you think he did that?

Model: He knew a dangerous amount of truth.

Director: So he spoke to others the way we speak to children?

Model: Yes, we play down to their level.

Director: Do you honestly believe philosophers are so far above the common man?

Model: In many ways they're beneath. And when they are, they look up and play dumb.

Director: How so?

Model: They pretend they can't see what goes on in the heights.

Director: The heights of high fashion, for instance?

Model: Sure. You don't do it with me, but if I brought you to a shoot, you'd have to play dumb to all the models gathered there.

Director: Why not talk to them as equals, but tell them I'm not impressed if I see they're full of sarcastic rot?

Model: You might find a few who listen. But for the most part? They'd come to hate you, and work you whatever harm they can.

- BOTH WAYS, SALVATION

Director: Why would they attack?

Model: Because you challenge their belief.

Director: Which belief?

Model: Sarcasm. They think in that they have their answer to the world.

Director: And yet they want, in earnest, the benefit of their looks.

Model: They do and they don't. Sarcasm is a sign of the don't.

Director: They want to have it both ways. How awful. I'd like to disabuse them of that.

Model: Good luck. Philosophy that doesn't take into account both ways is no philosophy to them.

Director: Maybe you're the one to explode their belief that sarcasm is the answer.

Model: How?

Director: Appeal to their better natures.

Model: Who's the optimistic democrat now? You assume we all have good natures at heart?

Director: No, some are too far gone—and may have started that way, for all I know. You have to find the ones that stand a chance.

Model: Stand a chance?

Director: To be saved.

Model: How would I save them?

Director: By calling sarcasm what it is. Or, if there are other problems besides, calling them what they are, too.

Model: The truth shall set you free?

Director: The truth might open your eyes. But then you must set yourself free.

Model: How many of the beautiful do you think I can save?

Director: One, maybe two.

Model: But then is it worth it?

Director: One or two lives? Of course it's worth it!

Model: You're right. These people will be my friends. Friends aren't so common that we can do without one or two. With your philosophy, how many do you expect to save?

Director: With all my life's work? A handful.

Model: Are you satisfied with that?

Director: I have to be. Because this handful will ensure the future of philosophy.

Model: How?

Director: They, in turn, will seek to save more.

Model: A handful each.

Director: Yes, and so on.

~ ALLIES

Model: But if philosophy is so isolated, how can it have any effect on the world?

Director: Through allies.

Model: What's the difference between a fellow philosopher and an ally?

Director: Allies are half of the whole.

Model: Let me guess. Philosophers are destructive and then constructive, but allies are constructive only.

Director: That's pretty much how it seems to me.

Model: Pretty much?

Director: Sometimes allies destroy.

Model: Okay. But on the whole they're constructive, yes?

Director: Yes.

Model: And when they construct they're mocked by the sarcastic.

Director: That's often the case, yes.

Model: Why do you think that is?

Director: Because the sarcastic, whether they understand this or not, take everything down to the lowest common denominator. The allies want to go beyond that. And so they're mocked.

Model: What's beyond the lowest common denominator?

Director: Think of the scientific age. Scientists went beyond.

Model: They believed in what they were doing.

Director: Absolutely.

Model: And I'm sure they were mocked.

Director: Certainly. But then they had their triumph.

Model: These are the kind of allies you want?

Director: The allies today are a bit different.

Model: Who are they?

Director: It's difficult to say. They're just forming up now. But there's one thing to note.

Model: Oh? What?

Director: There are different varieties of philosophy today that attract different sorts of allies.

Model: You mean some are conservative and some are liberal?

Director: Something like that, yes—but with other varieties, too.

Model: What sort of allies do you attract?

Director: I'm hoping to draw the beautiful people to my side.

Model: Are you serious? Why?

Director: I love beautiful forms.

Model: But not as much as you love beautiful interiors.

Director: True. That's what you and I have in common. I'd like to forge an alliance here.

Model: What sort of alliance?

Director: One between philosophy and politics. It's been done before.

Model: How did it go?

Director: Look at the history of Western Civilization.

Model: Our civilization is the alliance?

Director: Yes.

Model: Some people say Western Civilization is the most murderous, exploitative civilization there has ever been.

Director: There's some truth to that. Maybe we can change it.

Model: Well, we're too late. Western Civ is dead.

Director: And now we're looking at global civilization?

Model: Of course.

Director: I don't see the 'of course'. I still think we'll have multiple civilizations.

Model: What will they be organized around?

Director: History, mostly. History is hard to evade. But maybe, just maybe, one of these civilizations will be organized, in small part—around you and me.

~ HOPE

Model: Isn't that a little... arrogant? We'll almost certainly fail.

Director: Almost certainly, yes. But then others might pick up the torch. How do you think Western Civ was born?

Model: I suppose you have a point. I just don't feel... worthy.

Director: Neither do I. But why should that stop us? Someone has to try.

Model: But what are we really trying to do?

Director: Save the world.

Model: Do we want to rule the world?

Director: Everyone wants to rule the world. But why should we be like everyone else?

Model: So we don't want to rule the world?

Director: No, we don't. But we do want to influence our little corner of it, yes.

Model: That's it?

Director: It's at least a start. What's wrong with that? Tell me, Model. What are we in this for?

Model: To make a better world.

Director: Why do we care about a better world?

Model: Because we have to live in it.

Director: Why else?

Model: We want to leave a legacy?

Director: Why else?

Model: I don't know. Why?

Director: So we can have hope.

Model: I had been meaning to ask you about that, whether philosophers have hope.

Director: Certainly they do. They hope their efforts aren't for naught.

Model: Politicians need hope, for much the same reason, I think.

Director: Hmm. Maybe that's what they need.

Model: Who?

Director: Your beautiful sarcastic rottens. They have no hope.

Model: It's true! They have exactly no hope! A little hope might change their tune.

Director: What might they hope in?

Model: A world where looks are born free.

Director: Free of expectations?

Model: Yes, free to simply—be.

Director: But it goes both ways. They can't use their looks to manipulate others.

Model: Without expectation, I think they'd be happy to comply. There's something very innocent about liking the way you're made. It starts to turn ugly when others project expectations on you.

Director: Can we take them back to their innocence?

Model: Director, I'm not sure we can ever go back.

Director: So maybe they're willing to fight for the beautiful of the future.

Model: They just might be.

Director: Good. Let them have their fight.

Model: Would you be willing to help? You said you want to draw them to your side.

Director: These people, despite their good hopes for the future, are not those I'd have by my side.

~ A HEALTHIER WORLD

Model: Who would you have by your side?

Director: Those who might be able to help with the problem of genetic engineering.

Model: Engineering of looks?

Director: Looks are an offshoot of a greater problem.

Model: Can you say more?

Director: Let's take a step back and talk about scientists. They tell themselves and others they are working for a healthier world.

Model: Don't we want a healthier world?

Director: We do. But the tributary streams to this river of health involve desires for wealth and fame. Some want one; some want the other; many want both.

Model: So they aren't really working for health?

Director: No, they are. And this is good. But the question is—health at what cost?

Model: What do you mean?

Director: Look at the field of mental health. Have you seen the numbers?

Model: Millions and millions of Americans are sick. But are you suggesting mental illness follows from improved physical health? That makes no sense. Mental health *is* physical health. The brain is a physical object like any other. So how can you ask 'health at what cost'?

Director: I can ask because our technical view of the body needs to be enhanced by a holistic view of health.

Model: And if it's not?

Director: Then 'health at what cost'?

Model: It still makes no sense. Good 'technical health' works.

Director: We're living longer. But what's the quality of our lives?

Model: Well, you're arguing for a truism. We need a healthier whole.

Director: And that's the goal of politics, my friend.

Model: Politics? What are you talking about?

Director: Politics, in the broadest sense, deals with the human whole. It tends to the human whole.

Model: And part of this whole is the scientists and their love for wealth and fame.

Director: Yes. Many will always long for wealth and fame. So it's up to politics to figure out how to redirect these people's drive.

Model: Reward them for working toward a healthier whole.

Director: Yes. Technical medicine is useful. But as the goal? It's a dead end.

Model: You're saying we can't let scientific technicians rule the roost.

Director: Yes. Non-technical medicine needs more prestige.

Model: And you think politics can do that.

Director: I do. Oh, there will be writers, theorists who'll make the case. But there's no substitute for a statesman who knows how to lead.

Model: You've stated the goal of politics. What's the goal of philosophy?

Director: To keep politics in check.

Model: Ha! You'd encourage me then keep me in check?

Director: If you got carried away, of course.

Model: What would carry me away?

Director: The promise of political health.

Model: You'd rather I support disease? I could always go back to my sarcastic friends.

Director: Tell me. What good is curing cancer if we can't cure sarcasm?

Model: Are you being serious? We need to cure them both.

Director: That's what I want you to be. The politician of *both and.*

Model: I will be.

Director: And be sure to be open to this possibility.

Model: What possibility?

Director: That sarcasm might cause cancer.

Model: Now you're talking crazy, Director. I can't follow you there.

Director: Okay. I had to try. But wouldn't it be funny if it's true?

Model: I don't find anything funny here.

Director: Ah, I found your serious bone. And it has to do with health.

Model: There's nothing funny about poor health.

Director: I'm quickly learning this is so. What is it about health?

Model: Excuse me?

Director: What makes health so special?

Model: We all want it, and we can all suffer from it.

Director: It's the ultimate democratic thing.

Model: True. Health is the great equalizer.

Director: And as a democrat, you think that's good?

Model: I do.

Director: If you had to pick one thing about equality to salvage from the wreckage of democracy, what would it be?

Model: Respect for all.

Director: Really? Even your sarcastic friends?

Model: They're not really my friends; and, yes, even them.

Director: Do they deserve respect?

Model: As citizens—they do.

~ Variations

Director: Well, I'll say this. Good looks are anti-democratic—at least for now.

Model: What's that supposed to mean?

Director: Not everyone has good looks, unlike the way in which everyone has a vote.

Model: And you say 'for now' because you think genetic engineering, or whatever, will make us relative equals here?

Director: Yes. But as we've suggested, there will be variations of beauty. Some will like blondes; some will like brunettes; and so on, and so on. Camps will form around the various good looks. And imagine the fights!

Model: Oh, there will be no fights.

Director: Won't there? Don't you know that in Byzantium there were actual physical fights and assassinations over who wore what colors during sporting events? Imagine what kind of fights would break out over the color of people's skin, the shape of their torsos, the length of their limbs.

Model: Well, you have a point. So what can we do?

Director: Maybe we make people unequal before the eyes of the law.

Model: What does that mean?

Director: Oval faced people, for instance, have full rights. Square faced don't.

Model: How would that help anything?

Director: People who want their children to be square would have to choose to sacrifice their children's rights.

Model: So everyone would be oval.

Director: Mostly, and so there's less fighting over faces this way.

Model: But then you'd eventually make everyone the same! All in the name of... peace?

Director: You're right. That's no answer. So maybe we give everyone full rights, but can take them away.

Model: That's what we do now.

Director: Yes, but maybe we take the rights away for different reasons.

Model: What reasons?

Director: For instance, if you fight over the shape of people's noses once too often, you lose your rights.

Model: I like that better. But we still have the problem of everyone bunching up into a handful of 'beautiful' looks.

Director: Who has the choice of look? The parents?

Model: Who else would it be? The state?

Director: Maybe the state has a quota for each trait, arrived at by referenda. So many are to be shaped like this; so many are to be shaped like that. Democratic body types, allocated by lottery.

Model: But would people ever vote to include less than beautiful body types?

Director: They might—because they believe in diversity.

- ZOOS, LAWS

Model: So what is it? Ten good looking for every ugly one?

Director: Who knows? Maybe the other way round. If that were so, what would this democracy do with the beauties?

Model: Put them in zoos for everyone to enjoy.

Director: Why not? They'll call the biggest zoo Hollywood and keep the beautiful there.

Model: We're talking crazy, but we're on to something.

Director: We may be. But what about rights?

Model: What about them?

Director: The beauties should have none.

Model: What makes you say that?

Director: Rights are meant to protect those who have no power—or at least that's how we conceive of them today. The beauties, if not in zoos, have power. So they need no rights.

Model: That almost makes sense. And it implies something else. People might choose to be ugly—or to have ugly people created, I should say—in order that they, the created, will have rights.

Director: A world where ugly rules.

Model: But there's something disgusting about this.

Director: The ugly will take advantage of the beautiful?

Model: Yes!

Director: Should the beautiful rule?

Model: No, they'll oppress the ugly with disdain. They'll probably put *them* in zoos.

Director: Then who should rule?

Model: No one should rule.

Director: Anarchy?

Model: If we can discover the laws of human interaction, we can set in motion a self-perpetuating society that requires no one to rule. Anarchy, yes.

Director: But the laws of human interaction would rule.

Model: Well, in a sense, sure.

Director: Sometimes I wonder if civilization isn't the rebellion against those very laws.

Model: You mean we knew them all along?

Director: All along, yes; all throughout human history. But we wanted freedom, freedom from the law. And so we devised... philosophy.

Model: Of course that's what you'd say.

Director: Philosophy frees us from the law.

Model: How? By proving the laws aren't true? How can you prove a law that's a law isn't true?

Director: Philosophy topples the laws. In fact, all it takes is one to fall and the work is done.

Model: Which law would philosophy topple?

Director: What's the most important law of human interaction?

Model: Ha, ha. I think I know where you're headed.

Director: Where?

Model: The law of attraction to looks.

Director: I would topple that law. And I am living proof that it has been toppled in me.

Model: And yet here you are, spending the day with me.

Director: You are an exception, as you full well know.

Model: And you do your noble work by seeking out beautiful exceptions?

Director: Please don't mock my important work. I'm serious when it comes to this.

Model: I'm certain you are! But I do take your point. It takes philosophy to free us from this law.

Director: And if there is philosophy in the society of engineered looks?

Model: We just might stand a chance.

~ Chance, Loyalty, Hate

Director: Engineering can make everything look alright. Technically, things are perfect. Or getting more perfect all the time.

Model: And no one wants to argue with 'perfect', so mistakes gain great momentum.

Director: Yes, they might last thousands of years.

Model: A society can last thousands of years. But that's not proof it's doing something right.

Director: Of course. And just because a society goes away like a flash in a pan, it doesn't mean it's doing something wrong.

Model: Well.... The trick is truly knowing right from wrong, and seeking to limit the wrong and perpetuate the right.

Director: Maybe.

Model: Maybe? Why not?

Director: What if right, by nature, is limited?

Model: How so?

Director: It might take thousands of years for conditions to be right, so to speak, for the right society to exist. And when it does, it's beautiful—but only for a while.

Model: A fleeting bloom.

Director: Yes. And philosophy has to play its part.

Model: What is its part?

Director: It has to prevent people from trying to prolong the inevitable.

Model: Because it's ugly when they do? I can get behind that. But what's philosophy's motivation? This sounds like thankless work.

Director: Philosophy feels a loyalty to beauty. It hates to see it marred.

Model: That's it? Loyalty and hate?

Director: Well, I'd focus on the loyalty if I were speaking with others.

Model: Does hate always accompany loyalty?

Director: That's a good question. I suppose we hate those who mar the object of our loyalty. I guess the answer is yes.

Model: Is there a chance we might do away with hate if we do away with loyalty?

Director: Maybe I should reconsider whether you shouldn't be a philosopher and not a politician. There might be a chance, yes.

Model: So the question is whether hate is uglier than loyalty is beautiful. What do you think?

Director: Loyalty to good things is beautiful. Loyalty to bad things is ugly.

Model: Hatred toward good things is ugly. Is hatred toward bad things beautiful?

Director: It seems it all comes down to this. Can hatred be beautiful?

Model: We're taught the answer is no.

Director: Are we always taught the truth?

Model: No.

Director: So what do we have to do?

Model: Take a chance on figuring out the truth ourselves.

Director: Why does that involve taking a chance?

Model: There's no risk when you go along with everyone else.

Director: Of course there is. There's the risk they might all be wrong.

Model: I'm going to say hatred can be beautiful, if it's directed toward the bad.

Director: What makes something bad?

Model: It seeks to destroy beauty. Can you go along with me here?

Director: With pleasure.

Model: Am I a philosopher?

Director: I'm inclined to think you might become a philosopher-king.

Model: How does a philosopher-king differ from a philosopher?

Director: The philosopher-king has to rule.

Model: Wouldn't philosophers if given the chance?

Director: It's very hard to say.

~ RULE, WALKING ON THE GROUND

Model: Then try to say it. Would *you*?

Director: Rule? I'd never be given the chance.

Model: Why not?

Director: I'm not well practiced in making people believe.

Model: Believe in you? Believe in what's good for the country? And so on?

Director: Yes, all those good things. They don't come naturally to me. They come naturally to you.

Model: But you can learn.

Director: Even if that were true, it's hard to beat a natural who trains hard for the win.

Model: What kind of training do I need?

Director: You're getting some of it here today. You're talking about things you've probably thought of before, but getting them out into the open helps you be more secure in what you think.

Model: Secure when I'm under attack.

Director: Right. And you will be under attack if you choose to run.

Model: Talking with you, saying things openly here—it has a certain effect on me.

Director: So what will you do?

Model: I'll speak openly with the electorate, too.

Director: Okay. But remember not to shout.

Model: Why shouldn't I shout? I think I know, but I want you to tell me.

Director: Reason is powerful in inverse proportion to the level of decibels involved.

Model: So the quiet voice of reason has great effect.

Director: On those who listen.

Model: I will always listen to gentle reason from you.

Director: I hope you don't forget.

Model: I will never forget.

Director: Good. But politicians are especially forgetful.

Model: Why do you think that is?

Director: Because they have reason to forget.

Model: Reason? Does reason ever tell us to forget?

Director: Sure. It tells us not to remember inconvenient facts.

Model: Ah, you're teasing. What's inconvenient about the facts?

Director: They force a lowering of one's self-opinion.

Model: I think politicians would do well to remember these facts—so they can walk on a level field with the voters. Too many puff themselves up and float up on high. Voters see that, and they object.

Director: Why do you think they puff themselves like that? I mean, don't they know what voters like?

Model: I don't think they can help it. It takes great strength to walk on the ground.

Director: Someone listening to us might say that's ridiculous.

Model: 'Someone' might say anything.

Director: Point taken. I won't let you puff yourself up, even if you come to find the reason why other politicians do and think the reason is good.

Model: There's no chance of that.

Director: I wouldn't be so sure. It's good to have a little doubt.

Model: But not too much doubt.

Director: Definitely not too much. Doubt should be a seasoning, not the main course.

Model: For politicians, at least.

Director: Yes, and for most of the rest of us, too.

~ DOUBT, INNER BEAUTY, INERTIA

Model: What's wrong with too much doubt?

Director: You never get anywhere.

Model: Where am I trying to get?

Director: Elected.

Model: And you?

Director: I'm trying to get to beauty.

Model: Do you doubt beauty when you see it?

Director: If I know it's beauty, no. But I don't always know until I ask.

Model: It's always inner beauty with you, isn't it?

Director: Not always. Sometimes I'm lucky and the inner beauty comes in a beautiful case.

Model: Do you think that's how it should always be?

Director: I have my doubts. For one, then the world would hold no surprises. Don't you like surprises?

Model: Pleasant surprises, sure. But I don't like it when I find a beautiful case with an ugly inside.

Director: No one does, even those taken by the outer form.

Model: So why isn't everyone like us?

Director: Because some people decide never to look inside, for fear of what they'll find.

Model: Sure, but sometimes the one in question opens the case for us, like it or not.

Director: Yes, that's a moment many of us fear. The ugly coming out of the crypt.

Model: Ha, ha. I like the image, even though I'm frightened by it at the same time.

Director: What do you have to fear?

Model: I'm not immune to the charms of the body. And sometimes the beautiful on the outside know enough to keep their mouths shut. And sometimes I imagine such people must be beautiful inside, too. It's what I like to think.

Director: Yes, we're all tempted by what we like to think. And it's especially easy to think what we like when the other is silent on whatever we might have in mind. That's why we have to doubt. That's why we have to ask.

Model: Ask if they are beautiful on the inside, too?

Director: Yes.

Model: How do we ask that without being insulting?

Director: Oh, use your imagination and come at it in a somewhat oblique way. Have a conversation. Touch on serious things. Don't you know how to talk?

Model: Models aren't expected to talk.

Director: Then break with those expectations. Don't assume anything here. You could be making a terrible mistake.

Model: This is what philosophy is, isn't it? The avoidance of mistakes?

Director: In a sense, yes. Philosophy doesn't like to assume, doesn't like to think what it likes.

Model: How is it possible not to think what you like?

Director: It involves going against inertia. That's the only way to make progress in life.

Model: So if we're stopped, we start; and if we're moving, we cease?

Director: Or we accelerate, sure.

Model: But can we keep on accelerating?

Director: Look at how life passes. In our early years, time seems to last forever. As we age, the years increasingly speed on by. That's acceleration if you ask me. And I think it fitting that we accelerate to match.

- STEADY

Model: It's funny. We don't have to do anything for life to speed up like that. It happens to everyone.

Director: Well, I'm not sure that's true; but I'll take your point for now.

Model: What aren't you sure of? That we don't have to do anything? Or that it happens to everyone?

Director: I'm sure of neither.

Model: You're not sure of much, are you?

Director: Oh, I'm sure of a few things. One is that the quick witted like to think they're clever.

Model: A politician needs a quick wit, no?

Director: It can be helpful, yes. But as they say, slow and steady wins the race.

Model: Yes, they say that. But that doesn't mean it's always true.

Director: I think it depends on what we mean by 'race'. I suspect the one who first said this meant race to be a metaphor for life. Don't go rushing around all crazy. Don't give up. Just keep on keeping on. And you win.

Model: You're probably right. But in politics there are real races. And just keeping on isn't enough.

Director: What more does it take?

Model: You have to get people to believe.

Director: Can't you be slow and steady in that?

Model: Well, if you're in a hurry they'll think you're up to some trick.

Director: Slow and steady wins the race.

Model: Everyone knows this saying. Why doesn't everyone follow it?

Director: They're impatient and they lack courage. Or didn't you know that steadiness takes courage?

Model: I think that's a very good point. People forget this fact all too easily. When someone is steady, you assume it's easy just to carry on—when, in fact, it's one of the hardest things in the world.

Director: I know someone who makes music. He writes a song a day and has been doing it for thirty years. Everyone thinks song writing is so easy for him. How couldn't it be when he has thousands and thousands of songs? Well, one day we were talking and he said each day he faces an existential crisis, a great battle. He has to write his song.

Model: Why does he have to write his song?

Director: That's what musicians do.

Model: Okay. So what does he do about the battle?

Director: He fights it. And he told me that some days he wins, and some days he loses. But here's the thing. He doesn't know which one is which at the time.

Model: What does that mean?

Director: He was talking about success. He thinks some of the songs are good, some bad. But then when others hear them, sometimes these things are reversed. So the moral of the story, so to speak, is just to carry on, come what may. You might be surprised.

Model: Yes, but I want good surprises. And I would prefer something good to any surprise at all.

Director: You don't think that's dull?

Model: Maybe my sense of these things has been affected by my looks.

Director: How so?

Model: I'm never surprised when someone finds me attractive. This, I gather, is, for others, one of the greatest surprises in life. I could say I've been robbed of that. But instead I see it as a good. I'm not longing for surprise.

Director: I don't buy it.

Model: What do you mean?

Director: It must get boring always being attractive. Don't you long for someone to have no interest in you at all?

Model: Not really. I do long, however, for people to take me seriously for what I am inside.

Director: Then let that longing light your political campaign. And who knows? You might be surprised.

~ INTRIGUED

Model: I'd like to be surprised that way. But, Director?

Director: Yes?

Model: I hate to say this, but you seem to be in a hurry to get me started in politics.

Director: That's because I'm leaving here tonight.

Model: We should make more time to see each other.

Director: We live a continent apart.

Model: But sometimes I come to your city.

Director: Let's get together then.

Model: But in the meantime? How can I start a campaign? I have no idea. Do I go to party headquarters and ask them to sign me up?

Director: No, I have friends you can talk to. I'm sure they'll just gobble you up.

Model: How are you sure?

Director: I've talked to them about you before.

Model: What?

Director: Of course. They asked me if I knew any promising comers and I mentioned you. They were intrigued.

Model: You never thought to tell me?

Director: I was getting around to it.

Model: And if you hadn't happened into me here?

Director: I would have called... eventually.

Model: Ha! Here you are in a great hurry to start me up, and there you were sitting on important information!

Director: What can I say?

Model: Oh, you don't have to say anything. I understand.

Director: You do?

Model: Of course I do. We need a certain synchronicity in life.

Director: I'm not sure what that means.

Model: Timing is everything. And sometimes we need a stroke of luck.

Director: I'm with you on that. So can I put you in touch with my friends?

Model: Certainly.

Director: You haven't asked their party.

Model: Their party is that they're your friends. With that in place, any party will do.

Director: Well, if you don't like them I have other friends.

Model: But you like these friends best?

Director: For you? I do.

Model: Then that's where I'll start.

Director: You'll have to make them believe.

Model: In me? Yes, of course.

Director: You'll have to help them believe in the cause.

Model: What is the cause?

Director: What we've been talking about today.

Model: I could use your help there. Why don't you come along when I meet with them?

Director: That's not a bad idea.

Model: You can be my campaign manager. No, my campaign director!

Director: Thanks for the quick promotion.

Model: Do you accept?

Director: I do.

Model: So that's it. We've started it today.

Director: I'll call them tonight.

Model: What am I running for?

Director: A seat in Congress.

Model: What are my qualifications?

Director: You're a famous model.

Model: Will that be enough?

Director: Others make do on less.

Model: Then I'm all in.

~ PRESSURE

Model: You know, sometimes I think if I were a little less good looking things would be better for me.

Director: Why?

Model: There would be less pressure.

Director: What pressure do you have now?

Model: Think of this race. What shame I'll have if I lose.

Director: Because we know most people are shallow and they almost always vote for looks?

Model: Yes. If I lose, it means there was a reason I lost—that something is wrong with me.

Director: You can't start thinking like this now.

Model: But I already have.

Director: This thinking might be the reason you'd lose. That's what's wrong with you.

Model: So self-imposed pressure is wrong?

Director: I'd go so far as to say it's a sin.

Model: Ha, ha. Now I know you're not serious.

Director: There is no pressure here—only the journey. And it's a journey regardless of whether you win or lose. So make the most of the trip.

Model: That's good self-help, Director. I didn't know you were in that business.

Director: Don't worry, my advice is free. But seriously, self-pressure will be the death of you.

Model: But here's a little truth. If I don't put pressure on myself, I won't even try to win. Or do you think it's possible to win with no pressure?

Director: Trust me when I say that others will seek to put pressure on you. There will be no lack of pressure to win. It just cannot come from you.

Model: They say I'm graceful under pressure, other people's pressure.

Director: I believe it. So be that on your run. But please don't let self-pressure in. It's anti-philosophical.

Model: What? I've never heard that before. How is it anti-philosophical?

Director: Philosophers don't put pressure on themselves.

Model: Why not?

Director: It gets in the way of thought.

Model: I don't believe it. Sometimes my best thoughts come when I have put tremendous pressure on myself.

Director: Excuse me for asking, but name one of these thoughts.

Model: Well, it's not something you can just name like that, out of context.

Director: Let's reconstruct the context.

Model: These are private thoughts, Director.

Director: Private thoughts, unshared with friends, are risky. They might be untrue. And if held dear, they might distort your soul.

Model: Are you really speaking against private thought?

Director: I'm speaking against private thoughts born of tremendous self-pressure. These are dangerous thoughts, Model. They lead to dangerous things.

Model: Like suicide.

Director: Yes. Have you had suicidal thoughts?

Model: I have.

Director: Because of the pressure?

Model: Yes.

~ GIVEN, CARING

Director: Will you tell me one of your private thoughts?

Model: To those who are given much, much is expected.

Director: Who expects these things of you?

Model: You do, for one. You expect me to run and win.

Director: Throw it all out the window. I thought that's what you wanted to do. I was wrong.

Model: No, you weren't. I'd like to run and win.

Director: But you have to understand it's okay, and maybe even good, if you lose.

Model: What's good about losing?

Director: One door closes; another opens. You won't know until you're there. And loss might put you in a better place than victory. Who knows?

Model: More self-help.

Director: Self-help is when you help yourself. You're not doing that right now.

Model: How can I help myself?

Director: By adopting a devil-may-care attitude.

Model: Is that the attitude you have?

Director: About some things? Yes.

Model: And you want me to have that about the race.

Director: Yes.

Model: Do you think it will help me win?

Director: Yes, but that's not the point.

Model: Of course it's the point.

Director: The point is that when you're loose, more things are possible than when you're tight.

Model: I... believe that's true.

Director: Good. And there's something else I want you to believe. You haven't been given too much.

Model: What do you mean? That I can handle what I've been given? We all can handle what we've been given?

Director: There's the democrat again. Yes, *you* can handle what you've been given.

Model: You don't think everyone has the potential to handle what they've been given?

Director: I don't believe in that potential, if that's what you mean. Some people are overwhelmed.

Model: But still, they have to try.

Director: My concern right now is that *you* try, Model. But let me tell you this. I expect nothing of you.

Model: Do you really mean it?

Director: Well, maybe I expect a little.

Model: What do you expect?

Director: That you won't kill yourself over some artificial pressure.

Model: But this pressure has made me who I am.

Director: Who are you?

Model: The model who rebels.

Director: Against sarcasm?

Model: Yes—with truth.

Director: Good. Since you've succeeded in this, I take it the pressure should now come off.

Model: Consider it done.

Director: Do you care if you win the race?

Model: I couldn't care less.

Director: Do you mean it?

Model: So what if I don't?

Director: So the pressure starts up again. You have to find a way to stop.

Model: Stop being what I am?

Director: I want you to stop being what you're not.

Model: Believe me, Director. I would if only I could.

~ PRETENDING, THE WAY YOU PLAY

Director: What's stopping you?

Model: I know how to act.

Director: What do you mean? You know how to behave? Or you know how to pretend?

Model: I know how to pretend.

Director: Let me guess how it goes. You really don't care if you lose. But you're afraid people will know you don't care. And so you pretend you care. But to really fool others you have to fool yourself. So you really do care. Does that ring true?

Model: Yes, it does.

Director: What's the way out?

Model: No pretending.

Director: What will you not pretend?

Model: I'll not pretend I care.

Director: But will you really not care?

Model: If I don't, people will know.

Director: Tell me. What's a sign of care?

Model: Diligence.

Director: Can you imagine being diligent without caring?

Model: Why would you bother?

Director: Because you hold yourself to a standard.

Model: Maybe I'll lose and maybe I'll win—but I hold myself to the standard, and so it doesn't matter?

Director: Yes, and you take satisfaction in that.

Model: The way I play is more important than the win. But people just say that. They really care about winning.

Director: Caring about the way you play takes effort, more effort than simply focusing on the win. And there's a reason why many don't see it this way.

Model: What reason?

Director: They're lazy. They want to win with the least amount of effort.

Model: Well, I'm not lazy.

Director: That's good—because I, for one, care about how the race is run. And I'll tell you something for certain. I'm not going to kill myself if we lose.

Model: 'We'. That's the first time I've really heard that from you.

Director: Is it? We will run the race. And if we lose, we will recover. You're looking better suddenly.

Model: The suicide lacks that simplest of words. We. No one with a living, non-pretend we kills him- or herself.

Director: Then I'm glad we're where we're at.

   - WE

Model: I need we.

Director: We all need we.

Model: I've been trying to go it wholly alone.

Director: I've been where you've been.

Model: We're really not islands in the stream?

Director: If we are, don't worry—our words will keep us connected.

Model: I like the idea of fighting together for a cause.

Director: You want to win the fight?

Model: Naturally. But there's more to it than that. Tell me. Will your friends be part our 'we'?

Director: That's up to you. And if they are, you have to know they'll be as much your friends as mine—and maybe even more.

Model: Why more?

Director: They'll be dealing with you quite a bit.

Model: Won't you be dealing with me quite a bit? Even more than them?

Director: I'll be dealing with you more than they will, yes. And I will be dealing with you more than I'll be dealing with them.

Model: Who are these friends?

Director: Gatekeepers. A necessary evil.

Model: You're friends with the evil?

Director: Only when there's no other choice.

Model: So they're really not your friends?

Director: No, they're friends. I didn't mean 'evil' quite literally.

Model: I have trouble with that, with knowing what's literal or not.

Director: So do I. So I feel a little bad I spoke loosely there.

Model: But you said loose is good.

Director: You're right. A little loose is good. Can you live with that?

Model: I think I have to.

Director: It's necessary, yes. What's that they say about necessity?

Model: Necessity is good.

Director: Yes, but they say necessity is the mother of invention.

Model: What shall we invent?

Director: A candidate named Model.

Model: This Model isn't me?

Director: It depends how you want to play.

Model: Can I play it straight and be myself?

Director: Yes, or you can pretend.

Model: Pretend this 'me' is me.

Director: Yes. It's all been done before. It just depends on what you want.

Model: Above all else, I want we.

Director: Then consider creating your 'me' with me. We will drive this
me to victory.

Model: Somehow this feels immoral.

Director: Well... maybe it is, a little.

Model: And you'd still do it anyway?

Director: All's fair in love and war—and Congressional races.

~ SINCERITY

Model: But I like to think of myself as sincere.

Director: Then think of yourself as sincere.

Model: But this means I need to be sincere!

Director: Sincerely believe in our 'me'. Then work it like a puppet on
strings.

Model: You want me to work myself like a puppet?

Director: Would you rather someone else did? But, seriously, we're talking about your candidate 'me', not the real you.

Model: I want them to be the same.

Director: Why?

Model: I can't believe you're serious! Don't you think it's unhealthy to have such a 'me'?

Director: Generally speaking, I think it's unhealthy to run for Congress. A little 'me' is good preventive medicine. But look, I know most models don't act, so this is a stretch for you. Still, I think it's worth a try.

Model: I really think you're teasing. I want my 'me' to be me.

Director: Don't you mean you want your me to be me?

Model: Whatever!

Director: Alright. Suit yourself. But don't say I didn't warn you. It's just that when dealing with the insincere it's good to have a little armor.

Model: The 'me' is my armor?

Director: Yes. You can be yourself within, but you're going to get shot at all the time. It's good stop the bullets before they penetrate your body.

Model: Well, that makes some sense. But who is this 'me'?

Director: It's who you want to be.

Model: Why can't I be who I am?

Director: Are you who you want to be?

Model: No.

Director: Well, while you're working on that, create the 'me' you can aspire to as you go.

Model: But I'll be saying I'm better than I am.

Director: And you will be striving to live up to the claim. Listen. Have you ever heard of having face?

Model: I have. It's especially important in China.

Director: Okay. Your 'me' is your face. Maybe we should try and find a Chinese philosopher to explain what this means.

Model: My game face.

Director: Yes. We all need a game face.

Model: Why?

Director: Because sometimes we don't feel like playing.

Model: Oh. There will be times I don't feel like running the race.

Director: Of course. You need to have a game face for that, one you can put on then take off when you're back with your friends.

Model: But I don't like the idea of being phony.

Director: When you go to the theater, what do you expect?

Model: What do you mean?

Director: Do you expect the actors to perform only when they feel like it? Or should they will themselves to perform their best despite how they might otherwise feel?

Model: They should perform their best.

Director: That's how it should be for you. And don't tell me there aren't days when you'd rather not be at the shoot, and yet you pose and smile your best to please the photographers.

Model: That's true. But it doesn't mean I like it.

Director: There are lots of things not to like. But if you can win...

Model: ...then I've just earned two whole years—of more of the same.

~ REIGNING BELIEFS

Director: You can say you don't want to run, you know.

Model: Just tell me one thing. Is the puppet really just the game face?

Director: Yes, it's all the same thing.

Model: Okay. I trust you, Director. I think we can win.

Director: And if we don't, so what?

Model: And if we don't, so what. Now what about philosophy?

Director: What about it?

Model: You're not going to get involved in all this without a place for that.

Director: Won't you be the philosopher-king of the House?

Model: Ha, ha. Seriously. Where is philosophy in this?

Director: We're going to question the reigning beliefs.

Model: What are the reigning beliefs?

Director: The ones that are so obvious they're hard to see.

Model: Name such a belief.

Director: I can't.

Model: Why not?

Director: Like I said, they're hard to see. But if we win, if we make it to the center of power, I think we'll see those beliefs up close. Then we'll know what to do.

Model: But what if they're good beliefs?

Director: We question them nonetheless.

Model: Why?

Director: Full disclosure. We want the people to know what they believe in.

Model: They don't know?

Director: We don't even know. It's like what we said about what they think. That's why we're taking this trip—in order to find out. It's a voyage of discovery.

Model: So we tell the people what they believe. So what?

Director: So they can decide if they want to keep believing this or change to believing that.

Model: We're doing them a favor?

Director: I'd call it more of a service, a service every Congressperson should perform. If they did, I think the nation would be better off.

Model: I think you're teasing again. People know full well what they believe.

Director: People believe to the point where they think they know. I would show them their 'knowledge' is mere belief—and false belief at that. But, of course, that assumes we discover false beliefs along the way.

Model: It's a good assumption we will.

Director: So are you on board?

Model: I'm in favor of dispelling false beliefs. But what if those beliefs are what made us win? Do we pull the rug out from under ourselves?

Director: I think we step off the rug first, then we pull it aside and show the rotten floor beneath.

Model: Why not do that before we win? Do it during the campaign.

Director: We can do that.

Model: Good. And maybe in the process we'll pull the rug out from others.

Director: Others? They'll probably want revenge.

Model: We can't live in fear of people who will probably want revenge.

Director: I agree. But it's easy to say we'll live that way. It's very hard to do.

~ FIGHTING

Model: We're going to take the fight to them.

Director: What do you think that means?

Model: We're going to find the reigning beliefs—in each individual.

Director: You're sounding like a philosopher-king.

Model: Good. That's what I want to be.

Director: But you'll be dealing with a great many people. You can't really expect to probe them one and all.

Model: True. But we can probe everyone we come in contact with.

Director: You're assuming I'll be by your side.

Model: Yes. Will you?

Director: I'll quit my job.

Model: What about your career?

Director: Do you think I'd miss this for any career?

Model: Ha, ha! You'll make a career of working with me!

Director: That's not a laughing matter.

Model: No, you're right. You and I will find the reigning beliefs.

Director: And then we'll challenge them?

Model: Yes.

Director: And that will win us votes?

Model: Probably not, in most cases. But those who feel grateful for learning the truth, they'll be people we can work with—loyal people we can work with, who will help us win.

Director: That all sounds very good. But I have a little experience with these things. I would say we're very lucky if one in ten feels gratitude. The other nine will likely resent what we've said. You can't win an election with one in ten.

Model: Are you suggesting we need to make these nine believe?

Director: This is where I have trouble. Most candidates try to get people to believe in them, the candidates. But we don't want that.

Model: What do we want?

Director: We want them to *know* we're best, best for them, best for the country.

Model: How do we persuade them of that?

Director: It's less persuasion than demonstration.

Model: How do I demonstrate I'm best?

Director: For one, you can show them you're not full of yourself. That shouldn't be hard for you. And it will come as a surprise to them, because the beautiful often times are full of themselves.

Model: So they're surprised. What then?

Director: You show them you know the issues.

Model: Many people know the issues.

Director: True. But you're going to describe how to handle them best.

Model: You'll help me with that?

Director: I, and our friends, will work with you on this.

Model: So I'll tell the people what I'll do. But politicians are always telling people what they'll do. It's very different once they're in office.

Director: You're going to have modest, realistic goals.

Model: No one votes for modest, realistic goals.

Director: Yes, but no one is as handsome as you.

- THE GOOD, THE BAD

Director: Imagine this. An opponent launches into sweeping rhetoric about great promises she can't keep. You sit back and smile, then simply say what modest things are possible and how they can be done. Who will win?

Model: I don't know who *will* win, but I know I *should* win.

Director: Well, with your looks I like our odds.

Model: What if my opponent is beautiful? And passionate?

Director: You'll have to show why passion in politics might be no good.

Model: But people love it.

Director: People love sugar, too. Too much of it is no good. You'll be steady, constant, reliable, consistent, sane. If the country isn't too far gone, you'll win plenty of votes.

Model: My candidacy is a sort of test, isn't it?

Director: Of the country? Yes, I think it is. It's tempered reason versus excessive passion. We'll see who wins.

Model: But can't we be passionate in our reason? Are the two really opposed?

Director: For most, they are. For you? They don't have to be. But your character is such that you'll reign in your passion and use it for the cause.

Model: Can't the others reign their passion in?

Director: The other candidates blow wind into their sails and fly along the surface. The problem is, their ships have no ballast. Any sailor knows what trouble that spells.

Model: I see what you mean. My looks will provoke them to blow harder, won't they?

Director: That's a good observation. I think it's true. They'll be infuriated that people like you because of your looks. They'll rage against this fact of life and lose.

Model: Why do people like looks? Is it really envy as we said?

Director: I don't know, Model. Most people with looks, I don't like. You I like because of your character. But I don't think most people are like me in this way.

Model: You'd like me because of my character even if I didn't have the looks, wouldn't you?

Director: I like to think the answer is yes. But I'm not sure. It's something about the combination that attracts me to you. I think this combination will make you a winner.

Model: Why?

Director: People sometimes feel bad that they like people solely because of looks. They get a bout of conscience. They know they're being shallow. But you give them what they want with a good conscience. There's much to be said for this.

Model: There is an argument against me and my looks, though.

Director: I'm sure there is. Which one do you have in mind?

Model: How will I work with my peers in Congress? Won't some of them resent my looks and poise?

Director: Of course. You're going to put everyone to the test.

Model: A test of their mettle?

Director: Yes, and how much hope there is for the future.

Model: I'm feeling pressured again.

Director: Sorry. You shouldn't, though. I'm just counting on you being yourself—good and bad both.

Model: You know my bad?

Director: I know you're a human being. That guarantees some bad.

Model: I guess I'm relieved. But what about your bad? And you know which bad I mean.

Director: I think the bad you have in mind is the obverse of my good. It's how I alienate people with my philosophical bearing.

Model: That's what I had in mind.

Director: So what should I do?

Model: Stay behind the scenes.

Director: Were you worried I'd go on television?

Model: Not so much worried as... concerned.

Director: Well, no need for concern. I'll take your advice.

~ ADVICE, MORALLY CHARGED

Director: I advise you and you advise me. It's healthy this way.

Model: We'll advise the electorate and they'll advise us. What do you think of that?

Director: That sounds healthy, too. But how will they advise us? Through polls?

Model: No, there's too much reliance on that. We'll just talk, actually talk to people.

Director: Don't all candidates do that?

Model: Sure, but we'll find the people who make good sense and pull them aside for real conversation.

Director: I like that idea. But will we make them promises?

Model: No. We'll just tell them we'll weigh their advice. And we'll advise them back.

Director: On what they can do to support the cause?

Model: Of course. But only if they truly share in the cause. We're not trying to take advantage of anyone. That makes us unique.

Director: Everyone else takes advantage?

Model: That's how it seems to me. Maybe there are exceptions here and there, but I don't think they ever win.

Director: They don't have our secret weapon.

Model: Who, you?

Director: No! You and your character and looks!

Model: There is a problem, though. I want your advice on this.

Director: What is it?

Model: I don't have a significant other.

Director: Maybe if you were running for president that might be a problem. But for Congress? I wouldn't give it a second thought.

Model: Why do you think it's a problem for president?

Director: The presidency is a highly morally charged office. Congress isn't the same.

Model: What makes for the difference?

Director: I don't know. Maybe people look at Congresspeople as public servants, and the president as their leader? You're willing to tolerate more in a servant than someone you look up to.

Model: Oh, that's nonsense. People are intolerant when it comes to servants. They often turn a blind eye to leaders.

Director: That may be. But haven't you heard of the bully pulpit the president has?

Model: The word bully says it all.

Director: It's moral authority.

Model: I've always had issues with authority.

Director: You'll be running to be an authority.

Model: I won't be a bully. That's for certain.

Director: Do you think people want the president to be a bully?

Model: Some people do, yes.

Director: Why do you think that is?

Model: They want to be told what's what.

Director: They don't want to be told what to do?

Model: Some people do. But most want to be told what to think.

Director: Why?

Model: It's easier that way. You don't have the terrible responsibility of thinking for yourself.

Director: Yes, but these people already have strong opinions. I think their leaders echo these opinions. It's only on other things that the leaders tell them what to think. Foreign affairs, for instance. Things outside the realm.

~ Bullies, Laziness

Model: I want to conquer the realm.

Director: You want to tell people what to think?

Model: No. I want to ensure they don't attack.

Director: Attack foreigners?

Model: No. Attack as bullies toward their peers.

Director: Because the bullies are a majority?

Model: Let's just say they sometimes comprise the dominant part.

Director: Why do they have so much influence?

Model: People are afraid of them.

Director: Are you afraid of them?

Model: No, and neither are you.

Director: How do we destroy their ability to attack?

Model: We bolster the ones they intimidate. We encourage them to resist, to suffer nothing from them.

Director: How?

Model: We erect a bully pulpit and use it to bully the bullies.

Director: That's all we have to do?

Model: No. We must stimulate belief.

Director: What sort of belief?

Model: Belief that the bullies won't win.

Director: This all sounds very good.

Model: But?

Director: But some people are too lazy to defend themselves. It takes vigor to defend the freedom of the realm. Some don't think it's worth the effort. So they give in, hoping the bullies will eventually go away.

Model: They never go away.

Director: You know that. I know that. But these people don't want to know it.

Model: How can we help?

Director: We can tell them the truth. They're lazy.

Model: Not cowards?

Director: Cowardice is really just a form of laziness, in my experience.

Model: In your personal experience? Are you calling yourself lazy?

Director: I think we're all a little lazy.

Model: So we can all relate. And if we can relate, we can communicate.

Director: Communication will make them take action against the bullies?

Model: I'm not fooling myself here. A few might take action. But a few is much in something like this.

~ BRAVERY, ANGER

Director: I agree. And that's why I focus on individuals.

Model: What do you do if you encounter lazy coward after lazy coward? Is there a point where you just give up?

Director: All we can do is hope, and tailor our message to those who might be brave.

Model: But are we running the campaign on hope, hope that the brave will constitute a majority?

Director: The brave are few; but those who like to think of themselves as brave are many.

Model: An excellent point. We need to keep the truly brave free.

Director: Of the many?

Model: Yes, and other things, too.

Director: Is it really possible to be brave but not free?

Model: Of course. Why, do you think otherwise?

Director: I don't know. Some think there's an inner freedom that comes from being brave, even if you don't succeed in being externally free.

Model: To live without outward freedom is hard.

Director: You would encourage people to keep on fighting for that freedom no matter what?

Model: No matter what.

Director: What's the first step?

Model: Before anything, you have to fight your fears.

Director: What do you think voters fear most?

Model: Economic ruin.

Director: Really?

Model: People need money, Director. What can I say?

Director: What can you tell them to do about their fear?

Model: I don't think it's my business.

Director: We each have to face our fears alone?

Model: In the end? Yes.

Director: Most politicians would promise to bring better jobs, things like that.

Model: Those are empty promises. Politicians can't control those things.

Director: But certain people vote for the promises.

Model: And then they get angry when they aren't met.

Director: It's strange. These people fear, receive promises, vote, then get angry.

Model: What's strange about that?

Director: They prefer being angry to being afraid.

Model: So what are you saying? Deep down they feel the their politician helped them?

Director: Stranger things have happened.

Model: But won't the people vote the politician out?

Director: The politician understands the dynamic. So he or she gives the people something to be angry at, something other than themselves. But this makes me wonder.

Model: About what?

Director: Whether the people are ever angry at themselves.

Model: Angry at their own faults? I think that's rare.

Director: Are you ever angry at yourself?

Model: Sometimes, yes.

Director: Then you're a natural ally to these self-angry people.

Model: Great. My allies are small in number.

Director: Don't worry. This is just the core of those who will vote for you.

Model: How do you know?

Director: Because people who put the blame on themselves, though rare, exercise an influence on those around them. If they're impressed with you, they might talk about you, and this might well impress others.

~ LEANING, BOTHER

Director: But tell me. When do you get angry at yourself?

Model: When I get lazy and lean on my looks.

Director: Most people can't lean on their looks.

Model: True. But they find other things to lean on.

Director: Like what?

Model: Their families. That's a popular one.

Director: Also their friends?

Model: Sure.

Director: But isn't it supposed to be good to have someone to lean on?

Model: It is supposed to be good. And if it's brief, it's okay. But there are chronic offenders here. People who never stand on their own two feet.

Director: And some don't just lean? Some are carried?

Model: Of course.

Director: If you were carried, and could tell them where to go, would you still be mad at yourself?

Model: I would.

Director: Why? You're going where you want to go.

Model: The thing is I don't much care for these people.

Director: They offend you?

Model: Yes. I would never carry someone else. So the fact that they do so willingly bothers me.

Director: That bothers you, or the fact that you're only being carried because of your looks?

Model: That bothers me most.

Director: What if you say, 'If you want to carry me, you have to carry my friend, here, too'?

Model: Who, you? You wouldn't mind being carried?

Director: I've never been carried so I don't know. I think it's worth a try. Would you feel better with company?

Model: I probably would. But there's a problem.

Director: I'm sure there is.

Model: What if we grow to like being carried? What if we never want to come down?

Director: We'd probably do things to ensure that doesn't happen.

Model: Like become career politicians? Don't you have a problem with that?

Director: Some career politicians are good. But that's not the role for me.

Model: Why not?

Director: It gets in the way of philosophy. If the choice is to ask an awkward question or to keep relations smooth, I'd ask the awkward question. That's not necessarily good for my career.

Model: Ask me an awkward question.

Director: Why do you care about me?

Model: You're my friend.

Director: Why am I your friend?

Model: You're not blinded by my looks and you say interesting things. That wasn't so awkward.

Director: That's because you really are my friend.

Model: Would you bother to ask those questions of others, those who aren't your friends?

Director: If they're pretending to be my friends? Yes, I would—and more.

~ Pressing, Smiles

Model: What more would you ask?

Director: I would ask Congresspeople why they run for office. If they say it's because they have a calling, I would ask what it means to be called. If they have trouble with that, I would ask if they are like Joan of Arc.

Model: They won't take you seriously.

Director: Yes, but I'd ask them if they're called by God. And if not by God, by what? And so on.

Model: Yes, I can imagine the 'and so on'. But you must know people don't like to be pressed.

Director: Some do.

Model: Why would they?

Director: They have more they'd like to say. But let's try it with you. Do you have a calling?

Model: I do.

Director: What is it?

Model: To be a leader.

Director: What calls you to be a leader?

Model: I think I'd be good at it.

Director: Why?

Model: Because.... Because.... Maybe I should have said no, I don't have a calling.

Director: If you don't have a calling, why have you entered the race?

Model: Because I'd like to lead.

Director: Why would you like to lead?

Model: Because I think I have the right character for it.

Director: What kind of character have you got?

Model: I'm even tempered.

Director: Are all the even tempered qualified for office?

Model: Well, no.

Director: What makes you qualified?

Model: I'm modest.

Director: Modesty is a qualification?

Model: Director, I take the point. I think I have to avoid the question on why I want to run.

Director: They ask it every time.

Model: I don't have a good answer.

Director: What if you say, 'I want to run because it's exciting—and I don't have anything that disqualifies me'?

Model: People will think I'm kidding around.

Director: Let them. And then if they press, you can say, 'Let's talk about the issues—and then you'll see why I'm here.'

Model: You know, that might work. And it might fluster the other candidates who will have phony sounding reasons. I'll just say it and smile.

Director: Good. And I think that approach will serve you well with most difficult questions.

Model: What's an example of another difficult question?

Director: What has modeling taught you about the political world?

Model: It's taught me not to trust false friends. Smile.

Director: Very good.

Model: Give me another difficult question.

Director: Will you take advantage of people who are attracted to you?

Model: No one's going to ask me that.

Director: They might.

Model: Okay. No, I just want their votes. Smile.

Director: I think it can work.

Model: So do I.

~ SILENCE

Director: Pithy statements are good. But it's the silence of the smile that I like best.

Model: I'll have to let it sink in.

Director: Yes. People will be impressed.

Model: They know it takes a lot of confidence to be silent like that.

Director: I agree. But can you say why?

Model: Because when you're silent the pressure builds on you.

Director: Because people expect you to speak?

Model: Yes. Most people chatter just to fill the gaps.

Director: Does it make them uncomfortable when others don't talk?

Model: Often times, yes.

Director: What kind of person grows uncomfortable?

Model: The kind that's afraid to be alone.

Director: What's to fear?

Model: I don't know. I've never been afraid of being by myself. Have you?

Director: No. So I don't know, either. But I can guess. They suffered some kind of trauma to their reason. So when they're alone, and reason's quiet voice chatters away—they run.

Model: How can you suffer trauma to your reason?

Director: People may have punished you for speaking your reasons aloud.

Model: And so you learn to fear reason?

Director: That's my best guess. But I don't have to guess what your laconic statements with a smile will do. You're going to unnerve your opponent.

Model: They're going to feel pressure to say something to top me.

Director: Yes. But what can they say? You have a real advantage here. But tell me. You said the pressure builds. Does it build on you?

Model: I really don't feel it.

Director: Then you are blessed. But do you despise those who feel it acutely?

Model: I only despise them if they expect something of me.

Director: Chatter to fill the gaps.

Model: Yes. That's usually what they expect.

Director: Well, I think it's only fair. After all, you could just as easily expect silence of them.

Model: Funny how that expectation is almost never met. So I've learned to have no expectations. What about you?

Director: I expect people to be polite. But beyond that? No, I have no expectations of others. I take them as I find them, whatever they are.

~ EXPECTATIONS

Model: You can never know what crazy things people expect.

Director: Why not? Don't you ask?

Model: Ask? Do you?

Director: When I think there's a hidden expectation, yes.

Model: What are the signs of a hidden expectation?

Director: It's hard to say. I just get the sense they're counting on me for something.

Model: 'Counting on' is a funny phrase. What does it mean? They are taking you into account in their planning?

Director: They're planning on you, sure.

Model: I don't like to be in anyone's plans without my consent.

Director: Do you think your looks help or hurt you here?

Model: Well, I have it better than actors. People think their characters are who they are in real life, and they approach them expecting the actors to respond in character. I don't have any 'character' in my photos. So people don't expect that of me.

Director: Yes, but what about your looks?

Model: I think they might scare some people away. So no expectations from them.

Director: But those who want to come close?

Model: They don't feel like they know me, as they do actors, so they're cautious.

Director: Why cautious?

Model: I think they fear that the good looking will be cold.

Director: Are the good looking cold?

Model: Often times, yes.

Director: Why?

Model: It's a defense against those who are attracted.

Director: Defense? You mean the good looking are under attack?

Model: Almost always.

Director: What is this attack all about?

Model: There's something about good looks that makes many people want to be with you.

Director: Be with you and do what?

Model: I don't know. Sometimes I feel they just want you to be around like a pet.

Director: But many people love their pets. Don't you want to be loved?

Model: Like a pet?

Director: Okay. But even those who aren't beautiful don't have a choice. Don't you know? Love comes unbidden.

Model: They don't ask for their love for me; I don't ask for their love for me. No one's asking and yet there's love.

Director: Now here's the question. Would you be willing for all this love to translate into votes?

Model: Why wouldn't I?

Director: I don't know. Some people in your position might not be comfortable with this.

Model: I have no problem with it.

Director: Will you lead them on?

Model: They're going to follow me around anyway. Why not lead?

Director: I think that's a good attitude to have.

Model: Yes. But I won't let them get too close.

- WARMTH, SCREENING, REALISM

Director: But if they do get close? Will you be cold to keep them away?

Model: If they sense I'm cold, I'll lose their vote. But I won't feign a warmth I don't have.

Director: You really don't have any warmth toward them?

Model: I really don't.

Director: Hmm. We might have to surround you with people you can be warm with, and keep the others away.

Model: That sounds good to me. How do we screen for warmth?

Director: I'll do the screening. I think I have a pretty good idea what sort of people you like.

Model: What sort of people do I like?

Director: People who aren't overly impressed by your looks but love you nonetheless.

Model: But how will you know they aren't overly impressed by my looks? The only way to know is watch them interact with me.

Director: I can watch them interact with beautiful people who don't have your character. If they're taken with them, I know they're not for you. But if they're politely indifferent, I think that's someone you'd like to meet.

Model: That sounds pretty good! But how will you have access to these beautiful people? If they're lacking in character, they're surely not your friends.

Director: You can get us access. Have us invited to parties.

Model: But I don't often go to those parties.

Director: It might be a sacrifice you have to make for the cause.

Model: Well, if that's my biggest sacrifice I guess I have it easy. But what if the ones you introduce me to don't like me?

Director: People want to like those with good looks. They feel good looks and good character should go hand in hand. They're going to like you, Model. And if I'm wrong about some? No harm done.

Model: True. We'll send them off to the other models, who likely won't give them the time of day. But you know, I'm not the only model with character.

Director: I expected as much.

Model: Should we recruit them to the team?

Director: What would they do?

Model: I don't know. We can find something, can't we?

Director: Maybe they can help us raise funds.

Model: Yes, that's an excellent idea! But, Director, I don't think we'll need too much money.

Director: Oh?

Model: I'll get lots of free press. People love to take my picture.

Director: You have a point. And the lack of aggressive fundraising will give a positive vibe to the campaign.

Model: Yes, the campaign will feel warmer, more honest, more human.

Director: Guaranteed to bring in votes.

Model: Oh, don't say that. You sound so cynical.

Director: The fact that you feel that way will bring in even more votes. But please don't write me off as a cynic. Can't you think of me as... as... a realist?

Model: You can't even think of yourself as a realist!

Director: Why do you think that is?

Model: You're allergic to any sort of -ism—realism, cynicism, and so on.

Director: Is there no -ism that suits me? How about you? And what's wrong with realism?

Model: Realism suggests you deal in truth. But realists often sacrifice the possible.

Director: You mean realism can be used as an excuse not to do something.

Model: Yes, of course. And what's worse—realism often seems cold.

~ Optimism

Director: What's the opposite of realism?

Model: Optimism. Optimists are hopeful. They tend to see things as better than they are.

Director: So they deal in untruth?

Model: Just a little that they use as a lever.

Director: Are you an optimist, Model?

Model: Sometimes I am, and sometimes I'm a pessimist.

Director: You see things as worse than they are.

Model: Yes, I swing between optimism and pessimism.

Director: But doesn't this suggest realism is the perfect mean between the two?

Model: We can't live without hope.

Director: We can have realistic hopes.

Model: I suppose that's true. Can you name one?

Director: I think you have a realistic chance to win.

Model: Because of looks, character, and policy.

Director: And the people you'll surround yourself with.

Model: And they should all be realists?

Director: Yes. But if they have to err, we'd like them to err on the side of a little optimism. Campaigns aren't a place for pessimism.

Model: What will we do if I start feeling pessimistic?

Director: I'd get you out shaking hands and signing autographs. I think that will give you a lift.

Model: Why?

Director: I've seen you do these things before. You seemed not to mind.

Model: Not minding and enjoying are two different things.

Director: True, but you didn't mind those who only liked you for your looks. I think you'll enjoy it if people show up because they like your character.

Model: You have a point. That would feel good.

Director: And even if we lose, no one can take away your memory of feeling good.

Model: I'm feeling somewhat optimistic. But is it possible to take these interactions too far?

Director: The danger is that you start thinking they alone can bring us the win.

Model: What else do we need?

Director: To undermine the enemy.

Model: Judging from your grin I'd say this will be your department.

Director: I can think of a few things to help the cause.

Model: It's probably better if I don't know what they are.

Director: Yes, probably better. And you know, it's funny.

Model: What's funny?

Director: I'm somewhat optimistic here. And this quiet optimism of ours will go nicely with the overall tone of our campaign.

Model: I think other campaigns suffer from a sort of hyped up optimism that turns voters off.

Director: Yes. And you'll have a winning dynamic.

Model: What do you mean?

Director: As you build up momentum, you'll be unstoppable.

Model: How will I build momentum?

Director: You'll be off to a good start because of your looks and fame. You'll do well in the polls. But then people will start to see the truth of your character. You'll do better in the polls. This will make you seem strong. People will then be attracted to you for your strength. The more they're attracted the stronger you'll be. And so on. That's how you can run away with the election.

Model: And that's a realistic view of things?

Director: Maybe a little optimistic, but by and large real.

~ FRIENDS

Model: And your friends, the ones who'll get me started, they'll see it this way, too?

Director: I'm sure of it.

Model: But how can you be sure?

Director: Because I've discussed this with them. What's wrong? Would you rather we didn't have a thought through plan?

Model: I suppose you have a point. It just feels a little weird. But other than what you've told them, how will they know I have the right character?

Director: They'll get to know you. They'll meet with you over lunch, dinner, coffee, drinks. And then they'll invite you to parties. They'll want to put a lot of intense social pressure on you to see how you hold up.

Model: They'll be testing me.

Director: Yes, and I'm sorry but that's how it works.

Model: That's okay. I'm used to this sort of thing, social pressure. Though I avoid it when I can.

Director: Well, that's one of the issues. The social pressure never lets up in a job like this. Maybe it's not for you.

Model: If you're with me, I'm sure I can do it. And if your friends are even a little like you, so much the better.

Director: What about your friends?

Model: I don't have any friends. No good friends, at least. No one to help me with this.

Director: You and I will go out and find friends, and bring them onto the team.

Model: I'd like that. And they'll all be realistic with just a touch of optimism?

Director: Yes, that sounds about right. We'll just have to make sure none of them are star-struck by you.

Model: But, Director, what does any of this have to do with philosophy? Why would you spend your time on this?

Director: You might be the candidate who can challenge beliefs. Do you think I would miss out on that?

Model: But do people want their beliefs challenged? I mean, who really does?

Director: The people who will be on our team.

Model: Sure, a handful. But what about the masses?

Director: You will challenge and some will answer the call. That's about all we can say.

Model: And what will the rest do? Ignore the challenge?

Director: Of course. They always do.

Model: So if we're talking percentages, how many answer the call?

Director: Oh, I don't know. One percent?

Model: That's it?

Director: That's much! That's thousands of people.

Model: And I suppose each of these people will agitate in their own sphere?

Director: Well, maybe some of them will. Others will keep their conversions to themselves.

Model: So, what, ten percent will agitate?

Director: Sure.

Model: Well, that's hundreds of people, I suppose.

Director: When you've been working the mines like I have, and have maybe a dozen people to show for a lifetime of work, hundreds doesn't sound so bad.

Model: Point taken. And these people will, in a sense, be our friends, won't they?

Director: In more than a sense, I think.

Model: Well, win or lose the election, we will have won the battle.

Director: I'm glad you're starting to see it that way.

- GOOD BELIEFS, DOUBLE CURSE

Model: I have to ask about something that's been bothering me.

Director: By all means.

Model: What if we inadvertently challenge good beliefs? How will it seem to those who hold them?

Director: Well, let me put it this way. How many people, as a percentage, do you think hold good beliefs?

Model: Maybe ten?

Director: Do those ten get along just fine with the rest?

Model: No, I don't think they do.

Director: Because the rest hold bad beliefs.

Model: Yes.

Director: If we challenge those bad beliefs and, say, ten percent drop them—wouldn't that be a boon to those who hold good beliefs?

Model: Any drop would be a boon.

Director: And if in the course of delivering this boon we get a little too aggressive and challenge good beliefs, too—can those who hold those beliefs forgive us?

Model: I suppose they can.

Director: After all, if the beliefs are good what's the harm other than some annoyance?

Model: You have a point. But tell me something, Director. What makes a belief good?

Director: It benefits the believer.

Model: That's it?

Director: That's it.

Model: So it's a selfish belief?

Director: Oh, I don't know. Sometimes people believe in helping others.

Model: True. But why do they have to believe? Why not just feel good about helping others, no belief required?

Director: I don't know, Model. Maybe it's because of the double curse.

Model: What double curse?

Director: Do you ever feel like a good thing can be a curse?

Model: I don't know what you mean.

Director: Your looks, for instance. Sometimes a curse?

Model: Oh. Definitely.

Director: Well, what if a believer in a good belief sometimes feels their belief is a curse? Why not stop believing?

Model: I don't know. Why don't they?

Director: Because they have two beliefs. The second one is that the first one, the sometimes cursed belief, is good.

Model: So for the sake of the second belief they put up with the curse of the first.

Director: Yes. We feel cursed. But we double down on our belief because we believe the belief is good.

Model: Is every belief a double belief at heart?

Director: No.

Model: You can stop believing the second belief and still believe the first?

Director: Yes.

Model: Why would you?

Director: I really don't know. Habit?

Model: The world is very strange.

Director: It is. But tell me something, Model. Do you have a double belief about your looks?

Model: I don't even have a single belief about my looks.

Director: You don't believe they're good?

Model: Good for me? No. And I don't believe they're bad for me, either. They just... are.

Director: More things in this world should just be... are.

Model: I think people's beliefs should just be 'are'. No double belief; just a single belief. And there's an advantage here.

Director: Oh?

Model: The second belief prevents a clear analysis—of just how beneficial the main belief really is.

- BENEFIT, CHANGE, MISLED

Director: Tell me. If belief is simply an 'is', what happens when we ask, 'Why is?'

Model: Here, let me help you speak English. Why the belief? It comes with benefits, as we've said.

Director: Are the believers aware that the benefits come from the belief?

Model: They must be at some level.

Director: What does it mean that they are aware of the cause and effect here?

Model: That the belief causes benefits? It means they are aware that the belief is useful.

Director: And if the belief stops being useful?

Model: Then they ask, 'Why is?'

Director: What kind of person keeps believing in the face of uselessness?

Model: An unhappy one.

Director: And what kind of person changes belief?

Model: One who conquers their fear.

Director: Fear?

Model: Change is scary. A new belief is a whole new world.

Director: Are new worlds always hard to live in?

Model: I guess it depends on the world.

Director: What if you were told by a beautiful human being that a new world awaits, and that the adjustment to it is easy?

Model: You could be sure that beautiful human being wouldn't be me.

Director: Why?

Model: Change is hard. I would never lie to someone here. If I did, I wouldn't be a beautiful human being.

Director: You believe in beauty, don't you?

Model: What do you mean?

Director: As distinguished from looks.

Model: Yes, beauty and looks are two different things. Looks are shallow. Beauty is whole. I believe in the power of beauty.

Director: Can we always tell the difference between looks and beauty? From a photo, for instance?

Model: Of course not from a photo. You need to spend time with the person in order to get the feel.

Director: Ah, the feel. That makes sense. Will the voters feel you're good?

Model: I like to think they will.

Director: And if you're good, you're not someone who would mislead them.

Model: True.

Director: Do you think there's a significant group of voters who want to be misled?

Model: An interesting question. But there's another question we have to answer first. Are they aware they're being misled? In other words, might they not think they're being well led even though they're being misled? I mean, no one wants to be misled.

Director: Yes, I think what you're saying makes sense. They want to believe they're being well led, led according to their false beliefs. So there's well led and 'well led'.

Model: Precisely.

~ LEADERSHIP, DOUBLE ATTRACTION

Director: Now, you know, your looks and character will only get you in the door. From there you have to lead.

Model: But do Congresspeople have to lead? Don't they focus on service to their constituents?

Director: Yes, but to get what you want for your district, you have to lead in Congress. Don't you?

Model: I have to persuade in Congress.

Director: That's what good leaders do. But how many Congresspeople are going to like you, do you think?

Model: Well, I imagine there are Congresspeople who are jealous of others' power. And I think they'd be especially jealous of someone who has power at least in part from looks.

Director: Their power they had to earn? Your power you didn't?

Model: I think that's what some of them will think. They'll resent me for it. But they don't know how hard my power will have come.

Director: How so?

Model: Many people like to project their beliefs onto people with beautiful looks.

Director: What's the effect of that?

Model: I have to disabuse them.

Director: You have to let them down.

Model: Right. That's hard.

Director: But if you share beliefs?

Model: A powerful bond will form.

Director: Is this bond somehow stronger for the looks than it would otherwise be?

Model: Beautiful looks. And yes, it is.

Director: Why?

Model: It's a double attraction.

Director: And those without the looks can only have the single attraction, the attraction of shared belief.

Model: Right. It doesn't seem fair, and it probably isn't. But that's how it is.

Director: We need to make the most of the double attraction.

Model: What should we do?

Director: The first thing I think we need to do is purify our beliefs.

Model: That sounds a little scary, a little totalitarian.

Director: No, I just mean we need to make sure we don't have any bad beliefs.

Model: What if the bond is formed on bad beliefs?

Director: Then your colleagues can hardly be jealous. We'll have an awful amount of work to do.

Model: First we work on ourselves?

Director: Yes, we always lead by example.

Model: And then we work on my followers.

Director: Followers?

Model: If I'm to be a leader, don't you think I'll have followers?

Director: The word follower is out of favor.

Model: It's out of fashion. But I'm an expert on fashion. So listen to me.

~ FASHION, FOLLOWERS, SUPPORTERS

Director: How do we bring 'follower' back into fashion?

Model: Well, why do you think words fall out of fashion?

Director: People are tired of them.

Model: Tired, sure. But there's a political aspect to it.

Director: I'm sure there is. What is it?

Model: Have you noticed that it's okay for someone to be a follower on social media?

Director: I have. Why is it okay to be a follower socially but it's not okay to be a follower of a politician?

Model: Politically, we are supposed to be on an equal footing with our elected officials.

Director: And we're not supposed to be on an equal footing socially?

Model: We are, but we're not on that footing, actually.

Director: So if I have ten social followers and you have a million, I'm not your equal here.

Model: No, you're not. That's one reason I don't use social media.

Director: You would have the million.

Model: Yes.

Director: Let's get back to politics. I've noticed followers are often called supporters.

Model: Right, it puts them in an active role.

Director: To be sure, following is passive.

Model: Yes. The fashion today is to be viewed as active. Without your active support, the candidate will fail.

Director: What does it mean to support?

Model: You attend rallies; you give money; you argue in favor of your candidate with family and friends.

Director: That does sound active. So why are we saying it's just a fashion? Hasn't it always been this way in our democracy?

Model: We've always had supporters and not followers? And that's what makes us great? I suppose it's true. But I don't know history well enough to say for sure.

Director: Yes, but what about non-democratic societies?

Model: Well, they certainly have rallies. But they probably don't ask for your money. They just take it.

Director: But what about argument in support of a politician? Do you think there's that?

Model: No, I don't. Support is simply expected. And the expectation is backed by force.

Director: You're expected to be a follower.

Model: Yes.

Director: That's their fashion; we have ours. But fashion usually implies frequent change, doesn't it? Clothing fashions change each season.

Model: That would be a disaster in politics.

Director: What prevents fashion in politics?

Model: Steady government.

Director: Based on steady beliefs?

Model: Yes, I think so. Don't you?

Director: I do. But we've been saying you're going to challenge beliefs.

Model: Great political change happens once every generation or so in our country.

Director: So it's not a matter of fashion?

Model: No, it's not. It's a matter of survival.

~ SURVIVAL, SPIRITUAL DEATH

Director: But fashion for you, Model, is a matter of survival. It's how you make your living. But aside from your living, why do you think fashions must change?

Model: To sell more clothing.

Director: Why do people buy more clothing? Do the old ones wear out?

Model: No, not at all. They buy new clothing because they want a change.

Director: Something new.

Model: Yes, it lifts the spirit.

Director: Something new in politics could lift the spirit, couldn't it?

Model: Certainly.

Director: And you want to be that something new.

Model: I do.

Director: But you don't want to be a fashion.

Model: No, I want to be like a.... wedding dress.

Director: Interesting. You want to be something you wear once and keep forever?

Model: Yes, or at least for several years.

Director: When are you worn?

Model: On election night.

Director: And each election is another marriage?

Model: Yes, that's exactly how it is.

Director: But so many marriages end up in divorce.

Model: And yet we keep on marrying.

Director: We're a marrying country, which bodes well for you, I think.

Model: Why?

Director: When we re-marry we generally marry someone new.

Model: Are you suggesting I'll be someone new come each election?

Director: Yes. You're going to evolve as you learn. You'll shed old beliefs and grow new ones. This will happen just as the electorate starts to get tired of the old you. It's how you'll survive—politically, of course.

Model: Of course. But how can you be sure I'll grow new beliefs?

Director: When you lose a belief it creates a sort of vacuum. Nature abhors a vacuum. Something almost always rushes in.

Model: Another belief.

Director: Yes.

Model: But you say something 'almost' always rushes in. When doesn't it?

Director: When something is very wrong.

Model: Illness?

Director: Sure, or worse.

Model: What 'worse'?

Director: Spiritual death.

Model: The spiritually dead, are they ghouls with no soul?

Director: I wouldn't call them ghouls. I'd simply call them unfortunate.

Model: Why can't they believe?

Director: Because they've seen what belief can do. It can blind.

Model: If they've seen that, why are they unfortunate?

Director: Because they've seen it about dominant beliefs.

Model: I still don't understand. I would envy someone who could see like that. I would want to learn from them.

Director: As would I. But these people many times are terribly isolated. And that brings with it its own type of trouble.

- ISOLATION, LEARNING

Model: I would guess isolation is how they survive.

Director: Because they don't get knocked around by the believers that way? I think there's truth in that. But they have to use their isolation to grow strong.

Model: I agree.

Director: Good. Because, Model, for all your fame—I think you're rather isolated.

Model: I... am.

Director: And we're talking about taking you out of hiding and throwing you into the political mix.

Model: That's why I need a strong inner circle of supporters like you. But I'll always be isolated, you know—or insulated, at least.

Director: Why?

Model: It's in the nature of beauty.

Director: I don't understand.

Model: When everybody wants you, you have to defend yourself from the crush. I learned this at an early age. You see, I've been beautiful throughout my whole life. Beautiful baby, beautiful child, beautiful teen, beautiful young adult. So my whole life I've had to protect myself. Some models are luckier, in a way. They were ugly until they grew into their beauty. They knew a time when everyone didn't want them. You can learn much from such times.

Director: I don't doubt you. But what haven't you learned?

Model: How to trust. How to have friends. How not to be afraid.

Director: Well, you've already taken the first step. You know what you're dealing with. Philosophy can help you here.

Model: How?

Director: If you know something, do you trust that you know it?

Model: By definition, yes of course.

Director: Philosophy can help you know. If you know something about a person, really know it—do you think you can decide if you want them as a friend?

Model: Definitely.

Director: Philosophy can help you know people. But the last thing you need to learn, how not to be afraid, that will take time.

Model: Why?

Director: You have to come to trust yourself and your instincts.

Model: I thought you were going to say I need to come to trust my knowledge.

Director: Yes, but here's the thing. We want your instincts to be based upon your knowledge.

Model: Learned instinct?

Director: Yes.

Model: Replacing native instinct?

Director: 'Replace' might be too strong a word. I think we want to find a way to enhance native instinct.

Model: I like that better.

Director: That's good. But why?

Model: Because at the end of the day, what do we have? What has always been with us? Our instincts.

Director: Yes, but like beliefs, instincts can be bad.

Model: Then why enhance them?

Director: Because by enhancing them we can make them good.

Model: How does that work?

Director: Your instinct is to hide. We enhance this instinct and turn you into someone who knows how to make yourself scarce in order to drive up your price.

Model: I'd like that. In fact, I do that already with my career. I don't take on a lot of work.

Director: Yes, I've noticed. So here's the thing. Most people are sick of the candidates by the time the election comes. We don't want them to grow sick of you. We want them to want more of you. Vote for you and they get more.

~ THE TRICK

Model: That's the trick, isn't it?

Director: That's one of the tricks, sure.

Model: What's another trick?

Director: Most politicians are viewed as everyone's friend.

Model: I'm not that way.

Director: Yes, and it's to your advantage. People will long to have friendships with you.

Model: But if I turn them down, won't they resent me?

Director: Don't turn them down, but don't take them up. Leave them in limbo.

Model: You mean, let them believe they're my friend.

Director: A false belief?

Model: Not necessarily. Political friendships are different than personal friendships. These people can be my political friends.

Director: I'm glad that's how you see it.

Model: It's easy for me to see. I have modeling friends who aren't my personal friends. The principle is the same.

Director: Yes, and in order for you to succeed you're going to need to have political principles that people can see.

Model: What kind of principles?

Director: The sort that help you choose your friends.

Model: Okay. What are they?

Director: You never choose someone with manifest false beliefs.

Model: But I'll choose those with hidden false beliefs?

Director: Well, that doesn't seem so good. I guess we have to say you never choose as a friend someone with false beliefs.

Model: How many people have no false beliefs?

Director: Not many?

Model: You pretend like you don't know!

Director: Alright, very few. I guess we're going to have to focus on important beliefs.

Model: How many people have no false important beliefs?

Director: Few.

Model: How do we reach these few?

Director: You mean, you don't think they should reach us?

Model: I think if I'm a candidate, I need to reach out to them.

Director: Then talk publicly about your true important beliefs.

Model: And since these beliefs can help them they'll respond?

Director: Unless they're shy.

Model: How do I reach them if they're shy?

Director: How did I reach you?

Model: We met by chance.

Director: At a cocktail party, yes. Why were you there?

Model: My agent strongly advised I come. Why were you there?

Director: My boss couldn't come and sent me in his place.

Model: Why did he want you there?

Director: To represent our firm.

Model: What were you trying to sell?

Director: Operations consulting for Fashion Week.

Model: Funny, but I don't even know—did your firm win out?

Director: No.

Model: Why not?

Director: My boss says it's because I wasn't aggressive enough.

Model: You spent the whole night talking with me.

Director: And you with me. Why do you think that is?

Model: The others were dead.

- ALIVE, FORGIVENESS

Director: Why weren't they alive?

Model: They didn't have the spark you had.

Director: What was the effect of that spark?

Model: You livened up my night.

Director: You livened up my night. So that made us friends?

Model: Yes. Friends enliven.

Director: Is it possible to enliven then stop?

Model: I'm afraid so.

Director: What happens to the friendship then?

Model: It ceases to exist.

Director: Friendship is about life.

Model: Very much so.

Director: How do we prevent it from dying?

Model: We treat it with respect.

Director: That's it?

Model: We also have to bring everything we've got. No holding back.

Director: But isn't the holding back the tease that keeps interest alive?

Model: Political interest, maybe. But not with true friendship, no.

Director: True friendship wants everything up front.

Model: Of course.

Director: And if the friends don't agree?

Model: Friendship can stand the difference. The friends agree to disagree.

Director: Can political friends agree to disagree?

Model: Usually they just disagree and then that's it.

Director: So agreement is more important among political friends than among personal friends?

Model: That's a funny thing. But I think it's true.

Director: So why don't you have more personal friends than political friends? After all, they're more forgiving.

Model: Forgiveness is rare.

Director: Why do you think that is?

Model: Forgiveness takes strength.

Director: And strength is rare, yes. What if you forgive your electorate?

Model: Well, I wouldn't need to forgive my supporters.

Director: Sure you would.

Model: Why?

Director: Some of them would be supporting you blindly, supporting you for your beautiful looks. Could you forgive them that?

Model: I'm going to rely on the distinction again—looks versus beauty. Beauty is alive; mere looks aren't. If they support me for my beauty, which includes my character and all, there's nothing to forgive. But if they support me for my looks? I'm not sure I'd forgive.

Director: Would you cast them out? Tell them you don't want their votes?

Model: Yes.

Director: Ah, something only the beautiful can afford.

Model: Do you think I'd be wrong to do this?

Director: I think it might make you lose. But would you be wrong? No, I wouldn't say that. But how would you know they only support you for your looks?

Model: I suppose I'd have to adopt controversial positions. The kind that would drive those looking only to good looks away.

Director: What if they drive others away?

Model: I don't want supporters who are afraid of a little controversy. After all, controversy is the spice of life.

~ CONTROVERSY, ROTTEN

Director: Why is controversy the spice of life?

Model: It gets your blood going.

Director: What controversy have you had in order to know that's true?

Model: I pulled out of a show because of leather and furs.

Director: And what was that, vegan fashion?

Model: Of a sort. People got very upset with me.

Director: But I'm certain there were others who were very pleased with you.

Model: That's true. And that's how it is in life. Some will be upset; some will be pleased.

Director: That's an excellent lesson to learn. And successful politicians please more than they upset.

Model: But here's the thing. You can't know in advance who will be pleased or upset.

Director: Polls can't tell?

Model: No, polls can't tell. Too much is hidden from the pollsters.

Director: People don't answer honestly?

Model: No, I don't think it's that. I think many people don't know what they think until the actual moment when they vote.

Director: What tips the scale in the end?

Model: It's usually just a hunch.

Director: A hunch about character?

Model: Yes, about what rings true.

Director: People want to vote for true character, don't they?

Model: I think they do.

Director: And they want to vote for looks, and character coupled with looks allows them to do that.

Model: Here you are, cynical again.

Director: But people do want to vote for looks, don't they?

Model: I won't deny it.

Director: So all things equal, they vote for looks.

Model: Things aren't often equal.

Director: And still they vote for looks?

Model: Yes, and that's a problem—because looks won't know what to do.

Director: What if looks surrounds itself with good advisors?

Model: How would looks know which advisors are good?

Director: What are you when you can't tell good advice from bad?

Model: Lost, at best.

Director: And at worst?

Model: Rotten in your core.

Director: Because the core is where we decide on good and bad?

Model: Yes.

Director: If we're rotten, what happens to the spice?

Model: The spice of life? Controversy? I don't understand.

Director: What happens when the rotten engage in controversy?

Model: It depends how rotten they are.

Director: What do you mean?

Model: If they're only a little rotten, they usually get crushed.

Director: Why?

Model: Because they're weak.

Director: And if they're wholly rotten?

Model: They don't get crushed. They crush.

~ THE CRUSH

Director: I don't believe it. What strength to crush do the wholly rotten have?

Model: They have many supporters.

Director: Who supports the wholly rotten?

Model: The rest of the rotten.

Director: I thought the merely rotten were weak.

Model: And they are. But when together they have a certain strength.

Director: What sort of strength?

Model: The strength of... rot!

Director: Hmm. Maybe we're using the wrong word. Maybe it's not 'rot'.

Model: What would it be?

Director: Evil.

Model: Yes! That's much better. The evil have a sort of evil strength.

Director: But do you know what's strange? The evil get much of their strength from the good.

Model: What do you mean?

Director: The evil don't let on they're evil. They tell the good what they want to hear. And they get strength in return.

Model: I find it hard to believe that many of the good would be fooled.

Director: It doesn't take many. You see, the good are like a small amount of yeast in dough. They make things rise.

Model: And that's enough to make the evil win?

Director: Yes. The other evil instinctively vote for them; some of the good are fooled; and when things rise, the undecided are swung. That's often enough.

Model: We need to win some of the good over to the cause.

Director: That's what you're for.

Model: They'll give me the benefit of the doubt because of my looks.

Director: Correct.

Model: And then they'll get to know my character.

Director: Right.

Model: And then they'll examine where I stand on the issues.

Director: That's what they'll do. But even if they don't like where you stand, they might very well like the fact that you stand. They want a person who stands.

Model: That's a very funny thing.

Director: How so?

Model: Standing being more important than where you stand. Don't they have beliefs?

Director: I'm sure they do. And one of them is that a leader should stand, come what may.

Model: People want strong leadership, leadership with character.

Director: That's what they want. And there's no reason they can't believe in you but not what you believe. They're grownups, after all. They know people have differences. But they won't compromise on fundamentals.

Model: Integrity.

Director: Sure. And honesty. And so on.

Model: Can you have integrity without honesty?

Director: Why do you want to know?

Model: I might not always be honest with the voters, but I might have integrity nonetheless.

Director: Well, let's work that out when we get there. I think it will take some time and experience to talk that one through.

~ INTEGRITY

Model: Let's talk it through now. I think I need to know this before I run.

Director: Well, what do you think integrity is?

Model: A consistency, an internal and external consistency.

Director: So if you lie, what consistency do you have?

Model: You might be consistent in the lie.

Director: Do you lie to yourself?

Model: You believe the lie.

Director: And that's integrity? Lies within, lies without?

Model: Lies within, truth about the lie without.

Director: Truth about the lie?

Model: Truth that you believe the lie.

Director: So belief is everything here. You're honest about what you believe. Is that it?

Model: That's it. Honesty in belief.

Director: That sounds like a sham to me.

Model: And it is.

Director: What is real integrity?

Model: Truth within and truth without.

Director: So how can you lie and have integrity?

Model: There are times when lies are necessary.

Director: Then there are times when it's necessary to set integrity aside?

Model: A leader might have to lie about the disposition of troops.

Director: Why?

Model: So the troops have an advantage.

Director: Let me guess. The advantage is true, so the lie about the troops is somehow true?

Model: Yes.

Director: I don't believe it.

Model: You think we should sacrifice the advantage?

Director: That's a hard thing to say. So we're saying a lie for the sake of something good doesn't negate integrity.

Model: It's the 'for the sake of something good' that matters.

Director: That opens many a door.

Model: I know. It just really has to be for the sake of something good.

Director: Something everyone wants.

Model: Yes.

Director: What if what you want isn't good? A loss of integrity?

Model: Of course.

Director: So we need to know that something is truly good, if we're concerned about integrity.

Model: We do.

Director: And what if we start down the path of lies and come to realize the thing in question isn't truly good?

Model: We tell the truth.

Director: Just like that?

Model: Just like that.

Director: Consequences be damned?

Model: If we truly damned the consequences, we would keep on lying.

Director: Point taken. Would telling the truth win you friends?

Model: Certain friends, yes.

Director: What about the uncertain friends?

Model: They might be outraged with me.

Director: Why?

Model: Because they still believe the thing in question is good.

‒ Things, In the Door

Director: Then doesn't it seem that in a campaign the first thing should be to establish what things are good and what things are bad?

Model: That makes sense to me.

Director: Do you think we need the benefit of the doubt here?

Model: What do you mean?

Director: That this exercise is worthwhile. After all, don't most people just assume they know good and bad?

Model: Yes, most people assume that, certainly.

Director: So people would have to be willing to give us the benefit of the doubt if they're to listen.

Model: Yes.

Director: People might be willing to give you a chance they wouldn't give others. Would you be willing to work with this chance?

Model: I would. It would be the best use of my looks so far.

Director: So far? What other use do you have in mind?

Model: Oh, I'm just saying. It may be the best use my looks could ever have.

Director: Would you go as far as to say that's the only true use your looks could ever have?

Model: Of what other use are they? They open the door. Then it's up to me to walk in.

Director: But that's not how all the models feel, is it?

Model: Some of them do. But some of them are full of contempt.

Director: Contempt? As we spoke of concerning sarcasm?

Model: Yes. They know their looks are essentially useless, so they have contempt for those who value them so.

Director: And yet they earn their living from their looks.

Model: And so they have contempt for themselves.

Director: What a terrible way to live. So our rule is that looks should only get you in the door.

Model: That's our rule.

Director: And once in the door, we have to establish what things are good and bad.

Model: Agreed.

Director: Do you think that will turn certain people off?

Model: Let it. I think it will be refreshing to many, even those who disagree with our assessment of things.

Director: Why refreshing?

Model: Because we're going to dialogue with them. We come in the door and engage with meaningful talk, not empty words.

Director: We don't tell them what they want to hear?

Model: No. We tell them in all honesty and integrity what seems true to us. And then we let them challenge what we say.

~ CROWDS, FRIENDS

Director: All from the comfort of their own homes.

Model: So we're literally going to walk in the door?

Director: Yes, and that will be our primary focus.

Model: How will we know which people to meet?

Director: My friends will screen them for us. But we'll have some good conversations and some bad conversations.

Model: And that will be enough? What about rallies and things like that?

Director: We won't do them.

Model: That would be... great!

Director: We'll get you on television, of course. But only for one-on-one interviews.

Model: You have no idea what a relief this is!

Director: And why shouldn't we do it this way? Who says we have to play to a crowd?

Model: Director, I'm so glad you're in favor of this. The crowd was the thing holding me back.

Director: Well, there will still be a great big crowd out there, and plenty of loud mouths to go around—but we'll strive to minimize their effect.

Model: Why hasn't anyone thought of this sooner?

Director: Maybe they have. All I know is that this is right for you, right for us. So that's what we'll do.

Model: What makes some people love the crowd?

Director: I guess it's the thrill of the cheer. Why do you think they love the crowd?

Model: That, and it's forgiving.

Director: Forgiving?

Model: Get that cheer and all is forgiven. Everything is alright, if only for that moment. But I want more—much more. I don't want to have anything to forgive; and I want everything to be alright for more than a moment. I'm willing to work for this.

Director: People will sense this in you. Besides, we don't want the crowd to swallow you up, make you a part of it. We want you to be you, and you're at your best away from the noise.

Model: But that begs the question. Maybe I'm at my best away from politics.

Director: I'd say yes but for the fact that you say you haven't got friends. Politics, our kind of politics, can bring you friends. What do you say to that?

Model: I say you have a point. But I never want to have a crowd, even a small crowd, of friends.

Director: Have no fear. We won't allow it. The inner circle will be small and will be your only circle of friends.

Model: And the rest?

Director: Political friends.

Model: But won't the inner circle be political friends?

Director: Of course! But personal friends, too.

Model: How will I know they're personal friends?

Director: You'll find out after it's all over and you're out of office. They'll still be there for you.

Model: Why would they?

Director: Because they love you for who you are.

Model: How can you be so certain?

Director: I love you for who you are. I am confident my political friends will love you for who you are. And I'm not taking much of a chance in saying I think their close friends will do the same. If I'm wrong about them, I'm sorry. We'll find you better friends.

Model: Is it that easy for you to find friends?

Director: With you as the bait? The answer is yes.

Model: Please don't call me bait.

Director: I'm sorry about that. But sometimes it is what it is.

~ Friends Again

Model: You really think of me as bait?

Director: I think of your looks as bait. I think of you as human and a friend.

Model: And it's my character that makes the difference.

Director: Yes, your character and your mind.

Model: What about my mind?

Director: You're intelligent and you're open to philosophy.

Model: What if I were unintelligent but open to philosophy?

Director: You'd still be a friend of the cause, but not the candidate you are.

Model: If I weren't open to philosophy, would I be your friend?

Director: Perhaps a political friend, but not a personal friend.

Model: You limit your personal friends to those open to philosophy?

Director: And it's an exclusive club, judging from how few there are.

Model: Your political friends, the ones you want to introduce me to—are they open to philosophy?

Director: They're really just fellow travelers.

Model: But you said they would be my personal friends.

Director: Maybe I was wrong.

Model: What if my only personal friend in all this is you?

Director: I'd be honored.

Model: Be serious.

Director: I am. I think one of the secret themes of our campaign will be the search for personal friends.

Model: Why secret?

Director: Because if we announce we're looking for friends we'll offend those who come forward to be our friends but aren't.

Model: Oh, of course. Do you think being on a campaign is to our advantage in this search? I'd think the campaign might cause us to lose our focus.

Director: Yes, I know what you mean. But when you truly long for friends you tend to stay focused, regardless of what else is going on.

Model: Is it all really worth it for the sake of just a few friends?

Director: It would all really be worth it for the sake of just one friend.

Model: You honestly believe that?

Director: Look at how I've lived my life. Do you believe it?

Model: I do. But I have a nagging question. Why haven't we seen more of one another?

Director: The time wasn't right. Synchronicity, remember?

Model: But is that really it? Is that all there is to say?

Director: I think it says much. So remember, when we meet nice people and it doesn't work out, it just might be that the time isn't right. So we'll leave the door open and hope to see them again someday.

Model: You have a way of making it sound so simple.

Director: That's because I look to the truth, and the truth is often simple.

Model: When is it not?

Director: When people have bad beliefs that go against the truth.

Model: So we're going to try to simplify things in our campaign?

Director: We're not going to try. We're going to do.

~ DOING, PRUDENCE

Model: What are we going to do? Take away bad beliefs?

Director: We're not going to play to those beliefs like the other candidates do.

Model: And that will simplify things?

Director: A great deal.

Model: How?

Director: Our message will be straight, not bent.

Model: We're going to tell it like it is?

Director: As much as we can.

Model: What will stop us from going all the way?

Director: We ourselves.

Model: Because we're afraid.

Director: Better to say prudent.

Model: And if I say prudence be damned?

Director: You might fly too close to the sun.

Model: So how do we formulate our prudence?

Director: We find the worst of the bad beliefs and judge how far we can go against them.

Model: What makes them the worst?

Director: They deviate furthest from truth. And, as it so happens, those are exactly the kinds of beliefs people get most violent about.

Model: Funny how that works. Violence is the only thing that sustains them. But what's appealing to these people about these beliefs? What's so good about lies?

Director: I've often wondered that myself. Maybe reality seems so bad?

Model: Or maybe they want something very badly but can't admit it, so they insist on a false belief related to that thing?

Director: Could be.

Model: Believing this way is a kind of doing, isn't it?

Director: What kind of doing?

Model: Doing harm to the truth.

Director: Do you think our unbelief is a kind of doing, doing justice to the truth?

Model: Justice, yes. Justice gives each thing what it deserves. The ultimate thing we deserve is the truth. But not some of the truth. All of the truth.

Director: So it's not enough not to believe?

Model: We must call the belief what it is—a lie. That's what we do.

Director: But within the limits of prudence?

Model: Prudence means fighting but living to fight another day, right?

Director: Yes.

Model: Well, we can't destroy ourselves in the fight. We'll go as far as we can. And later we'll try again.

Director: Because times can change.

Model: They certainly can.

Director: Can we do something to change them?

Model: We can persuade people to fight the lies. But this has to be within prudence. A backlash might follow otherwise and make things worse.

Director: Do you think there will be a backlash to your campaign?

Model: It depends how we run it.

Director: Maybe we should be bold in private but reserved in public.

Model: By private you mean when we meet with others one-on-one or only with a few.

Director: Yes. And I know that's really a sort of hybrid of public and private, but I think you know what I mean.

Model: I do. And I think you're right. Our private supporters will know why we're reserved in public. They'll be reserved in public, too.

Director: And they'll admire what we're doing.

Model: Telling the truth, or at least not supporting powerful lies? Yes, they will.

- THE LIE

Director: What do you think is the most powerful lie?

Model: In a democracy? It's the opposite of the most powerful truth. What do you think is the most powerful lie?

Director: I'm waiting to see what we learn on the campaign.

Model: What about the most powerful truth? Also waiting on that?

Director: Yes.

Model: Fair enough. But I have a suspicion about what this truth is.

Director: What is it?

Model: The truth is that the best don't rule.

Director: Why not?

Model: They aren't appreciated for what they are.

Director: So what does it mean if you, Model, come to rule? Does it mean you can't be the best?

Model: You tell me.

Director: I think you are among the best. And I think you can rule. But this will be a watershed moment.

Model: Why?

Director: Because you don't believe the lies.

Model: You don't, either.

Director: This makes our joining forces special.

Model: Politics and philosophy. What's the goal of philosophy?

Director: To allow for a better world. What's the goal of politics?

Model: To create a better world. Very similar.

Director: Yes. So let me tell you something I sometimes wonder. If the times were right, would philosophers be politicians? In other words, would they have never come to philosophy? Plato suggests as much in one of his letters.

Model: What does he say?

Director: He had a youthful passion for politics. But when he got up close and saw how the game was played during the time he lived in, he wanted nothing to do with it. And so he turned to philosophy. I'm sure that's a simplification, but it is the gist of how things go, I'm persuaded to think.

Model: You would have been a politician in another age?

Director: Don't seem so surprised! I might have had great political skills. Who knows?

Model: But the times are good enough for the lowly likes of me.

Director: You know I don't mean it that way. The time is right for you, beautiful you.

‐ OUR TIMES, CAUTION, FORTUNE

Model: Tell me the truth about our times.

Director: We live in interesting times. 'May you live in interesting times' is an old curse, you know.

Model: What makes the times interesting?

Director: People falling away from old beliefs. But this makes some believe all the more. Thus there is tension, terrible tension. And this tension can lead to upheaval. Everything depends on how this tension is addressed.

Model: We have to be prudent.

Director: Yes, but not to a fault. We must be bold, but bold within reason. Your character is such that you won't get carried away. But I, and others, will need to encourage you.

Model: Thanks. Now you're saying I'm cowardly.

Director: Caution and cowardice are very different things. You are cautious, because you don't easily trust. That's a virtue as far as I'm concerned.

Model: Are you cautious this way?

Director: I'm cautious in my own way. I ask lots of questions because I need to be sure before I commit.

Model: I don't ask enough questions.

Director: Don't worry about that. If you asked as many questions as I do, you'd put people off.

Model: So you'll ask the questions for me? People will tell you what they wouldn't tell me?

Director: You and I will have different roles. In a political campaign, no one person can do it all.

Model: Well, that makes sense. But do you think I'm deceiving them by not asking all the questions I have?

Director: I suppose if you come out and tell them, 'I am completely and unreservedly in lockstep with you'—you'd be lying, sure. But if you simply thank them for a wonderful talk and let them think what they think—what harm is there in that?

Model: And then you follow up and clean up my mess.

Director: Don't be so hard on yourself. What mess could you leave? If you were one of the other politicians, there might be a mess of ill begotten promises and the like. But you won't do that sort of thing.

Model: True.

Director: Besides, even if they suspect you're not telling them everything—that will make you seem deep.

Model: So everything I do or don't do is to my advantage?

Director: Why do you think I want to work with you?

Model: Maybe it's because we're here at a lovely island resort and it seems so easy to scheme to rule the world?

Director: You're right. Scheming is easy. Execution is hard. But the setting here is auspicious, I think. And we met by chance. Chance is Fortune in disguise.

Model: Do you really believe in Fortune?

Director: It's not a matter of belief. I can prove that Fortune has a great hand in all we do.

Model: How will Fortune adversely affect our campaign?

Director: I can't tell you that. Fortune will tell us when she's ready.

Model: Is there anything we can do to prepare?

Director: Keep things as simple as we can. So if Fortune strikes, we can easily make repairs. That's the major mistake of most campaigns. Things aren't simple, and then Fortune stirs everything up, and it's a major effort to recover.

Model: I find it interesting that you say it stirs things up. In a campaign like ours, stirring can be good. It can show how clear we are.

Director: Yes, that's true. But let's be sure we're up to the challenge.

~ SUCCESS, THEY

Model: Yes. And when we win, we'll simplify things for the nation.

Director: Yes, up to a point.

Model: What do you mean? What point?

Director: The ultimate simplification is to make everyone part of 'we'.

Model: Yes, I know what you mean.

Director: But is everyone part of 'we'?

Model: No, it's impossible for everyone to be part of 'we'.

Director: So there's always 'we' and 'they'.

Model: Always.

Director: What does it take to make a 'they'?

Model: One person.

Director: And one person only?

Model: Yes.

Director: Is this person good or bad?

Model: Bad. Unless they're a rebel for the cause.

Director: What cause?

Model: The cause of truth.

Director: And what is the truth?

Model: We are not, we cannot be, all the same.

Director: Why not?

Model: Because then all difference dies.

Director: So what?

Model: Difference is what challenges us to grow.

Director: So we'd be a nation of pygmies.

Model: But we could be so much more.

Director: What's wrong with pygmies? For all you and I know they live a very happy life.

Model: That's true. But we as a people believe in diversity.

Director: Why?

Model: We know it makes us stronger.

Director: Do you mean 'they' make us stronger?

Model: We, in our encounter with them, make ourselves stronger.

Director: But not if we choose to crush them when we can.

Model: No, not then.

Director: So tolerance is a virtue.

Model: Yes.

Director: And virtues are good because they make us stronger.

Model: That's right.

Director: And without this strength, tolerance would be of no use.

Model: It might keep the peace.

Director: True, for a time.

Model: You're right. Strength keeps the peace.

Director: Now tell me something. How does it feel to be tolerated?

Model: Not as good as it feels to be respected.

Director: Why is one person respected and another not?

Model: Because the one has strength.

Director: So if we find ourselves being a 'they', what should we do?

Model: Be as strong as we can.

~ RESPECT

Director: What good is respect?

Model: I don't understand.

Director: I mean, why do we want respect—at bottom?

Model: At bottom? Respect just... just... makes us feel good!

Director: And if we don't have respect it makes us feel bad?

Model: Of course.

Director: These are character traits, aren't they?

Model: What do you mean?

Director: When you're respected, it makes you one of the good of character. When you're not respected, it makes you one of the bad.

Model: That's the exact opposite of things.

Director: What do you mean?

Model: Your goodness of character is what makes you respected, not the other way round. And so it is with the bad.

Director: No, I'm pretty sure I'm describing it right.

Model: Well, it's a chicken and egg question.

Director: Not if you factor strength into the mix.

Model: How so?

Director: Strength wins you respect. Yes?

Model: Yes.

Director: Do we respect the bad?

Model: We don't.

Director: But we respect those with strength. Well?

Model: As we said.

Director: So those with strength can't be bad, because we don't respect the bad and we respect those with strength. The rest all follows from this.

Model: What a sophist you are! So if you have no strength, you won't be respected; and that means you're of bad character?

Director: I think it's worth looking at the world through this lens for a bit, even if we can find a better way to describe things. There are many people who think the weak are bad. It's only that they don't call them weak.

Model: What do they call them?

Director: Things that have to do with character. Unsound. Shifty. Unprincipled, even.

Model: That's because the strong are sound, determined, and principled.

Director: You will be a strong politician—very well respected.

Model: Because I don't say much.

Director: Doesn't it take strength not to say much?

Model: For some, yes.

Director: For you?

Model: I think my silence reflects my strength.

Director: I think it's true. So it's easy for you to hold your tongue?

Model: The image is wrong. I feel no need to hold it—nor to wag it, for that matter.

Director: Well, regardless. When you do decide to speak, people will listen.

Model: That's a lot of pressure.

Director: That's the game you're in.

~ Pressure, Honor

Director: But what am I saying? There is no pressure here.

Model: What are you talking about?

Director: Commit yourself to speaking only basic, simple truths. Let nothing else come from your lips. If you're not trying to say anything grand, the pressure disappears.

Model: What if people think I'm simple?

Director: Stupid? Hardly. Everything about you exudes intelligence. Do you know how uncommon it is for the intelligent to be simple?

Model: Are you simple?

Director: I try to be, even if I'm not.

Model: What prevents you?

Director: Two things. Vanity and fear.

Model: Vanity I can understand. But what's the fear?

Director: Being understood.

Model: It's funny. We want nothing more than to be understood; and then when we are, it makes us afraid. I guess we have to fall back on our prudence.

Director: Yes, prudence is the thing. But there's a certain pressure here.

Model: How so?

Director: We want to protect ourselves. But we don't want to become misers.

Model: Misers? What do they have to do with it?

Director: Don't you know? Misers aren't greedy. They're overly prudent. They think money protects them. And they want as much protection as they can get.

Model: Why is there a pressure not to become a miser?

Director: It comes from a generous nature. It's a sort of tug of war in the soul. Prudence on the one side, generosity on the other. The pull creates pressure. Or so it seems to me.

Model: I think you're right. But I don't feel this pressure. I guess I don't have a generous nature.

Director: Then beware. There's nothing to fight the prudence in your soul. Nothing except, maybe... honor.

Model: I care what certain people think. If you call that 'honor', that's fine with me. I care what you think, for instance. But I also care what I think about myself.

Director: That's the best care there is. And I would call that honor. You are an honorable man. And voters like it.

Model: You always bring it back to that. But, again, I think you're right. I would prefer to elect someone of honor over someone with no honor.

Director: How do you think someone gives in and has no honor?

Model: It's easier that way. I think it's as simple as that.

Director: Who do you think those who lack honor harm?

Model: Necessarily? No one, I suppose. But they make a poor example.

Director: For the young?

Model: Especially, yes.

Director: But aren't they helpful in a way?

Model: How?

Director: Parents can point to them and say, 'Don't be like them!'

Model: 'Be careful or you'll end up like them!' Ha, ha. True.

Director: Why do you think parents don't want their children to be like them?

Model: Let's be clear. We're not talking about being a liar or whatever. We're just talking about lacking that care for what you think of yourself?

Director: Yes.

Model: Then I don't know.

~ VIRTUE

Director: And you call yourself a man of honor?

Model: *You* called *me* a man of honor!

Director: Alright, so I did. I'll tell you what I think. Instruction in honor is the key to living a virtuous life.

Model: Why?

Director: Aren't you going to ask me what a virtuous life is?

Model: What is it?

Director: A life of self-control. Many models don't have that, do they?

Model: No, they don't.

Director: Why do you think that is?

Model: Because people let them get away with everything.

Director: Yes, but what's the reason they want to get away with everything?

Model: We all want to get away with everything.

Director: What stops us?

Model: Self-control. And honor gives us self-control. We care what we think about ourselves.

Director: Your models who get away with everything, what do they think about themselves?

Model: Some of them are disgusted with themselves.

Director: If you were a parent, would you want your children to grow up to be disgusted with themselves?

Model: Of course not.

Director: Why not?

Model: Because I love them.

Director: And you want good things for those you love.

Model: Don't we all? But what about philosophers?

Director: What about them?

Model: Do they love honor?

Director: Love honor? No. Do they have honor? Yes, in my opinion they do.

Model: What's it based on? Truth?

Director: Truth for sure, yes. But also on courage.

Model: Courage to be able to ask the difficult question?

Director: And not to be afraid to go wherever the answers lead.

Model: Where is the self-control in a philosopher?

Director: It comes in not thinking you know what you don't.

Model: Not jumping to conclusions?

Director: Yes.

Model: Some people see something happen once and believe they see a pattern.

Director: Yes, and some people believe coincidence is cause.

Model: There are many bad ways to think. It takes self-control to avoid them, doesn't it?

Director: It certainly does.

Model: And I think there's justice in this.

Director: How so?

Model: When we do justice to something, we know it for what it is. To know something that way often takes an effort of self-control to let the thing unfold in all its fullness.

Director: If it's a thing that admits of such fulness.

Model: True. But do you know what I mean?

Director: I do. And I think you're on to something important. Justice and self-control are linked.

Model: So philosophers are always just?

Director: I was just going to ask about politicians.

- JUSTICE

Model: Oh, you know politicians aren't always just.

Director: Then I'll assume you know philosophers aren't always just.

Model: When aren't they just?

Director: Are we saying justice is giving something what it deserves?

Model: Yes.

Director: Philosophers aren't just when they're overly prudent.

Model: They don't tell it fully like it is, and therefore don't give the person or thing in question what it deserves.

Director: Do you believe it?

Model: I do. But what about themselves?

Director: What do you mean?

Model: Do they give themselves what they deserve?

Director: What do you think they deserve?

Model: A university chair of philosophy.

Director: I'm not sure I would wish that on any of my friends.

Model: Why not?

Director: A friend of mine is a writer of philosophy. He once spoke with a philosophy professor at a famous university. He asked the professor if the professor might read one of his books and tell him what he thinks.

Model: What the professor thinks or what the writer thinks?

Director: The two questions are inextricably linked. Anyway, the professor launched into a tirade about how harried his life is. He has to read many books to prepare for class. He has to read peers' books before they're published. He has to read countless student papers. Then he has to write his own books. And edit them. And edit them again. In short, he has no time even to read a detective story let alone another book of philosophy.

Model: It doesn't sound like the professor is enjoying life very much.

Director: No, it doesn't.

Model: Maybe all the philosophy he's reading is bad.

Director: Yes, one wonders.

Model: But do you really think all philosophy jobs are like that?

Director: I don't know. I'm open to possibilities.

Model: Well, you have to try.

Director: I do try. I try to be the best philosopher I can be.

Model: Without reward.

Director: You think I deserve a reward? For doing something I love? Well, I do, too. And I think you'll deserve an award if you go into politics.

Model: What's my reward?

Director: Election, what else?

Model: But what's your reward?

Director: Oh, you won't believe me.

Model: Try me.

Director: Friends like you.

Model: Somehow, I believe that's really all you're after.

Director: I do want a little bit more.

Model: What?

Director: For my friends to grow in philosophy, if only a very little.

Model: Why only a very little?

Director: Because very little here is much.

~ MUCH

Model: Why is it much?

Director: Because growth in philosophy involves a very great struggle.

Model: A struggle of self-control?

Director: Yes. Though I'll let you in on a secret. Some philosophers want their work to appear effortless.

Model: Why not take credit for very hard work?

Director: Philosophy isn't about credit.

Model: It isn't? Then why not publish anonymously or under pseudonyms?

Director: Some do.

Model: Sure, but it all comes out in the end. Right?

Director: Sometimes. Maybe all we can say is that philosophy isn't necessarily about getting credit.

Model: What's it necessarily about?

Director: Furthering the cause.

Model: With my cause, election, it's all about me. Sure, it's about our team. But in the end it's all about me.

Director: I know you don't think that. I know you know it's about the cause here, too.

Model: Philosophy's cause.

Director: Yes. You and I are vehicles for the cause.

Model: Vehicles or vessels?

Director: Either or both. Is that appealing to you?

Model: To be a part of something greater than myself while being at once essentially myself? How would that not appeal?

Director: Good. It's about you and I and us, as well as the greater we.

Model: And like all good heroes, we need a good them.

Director: The enemy, yes. Our them. They call themselves good.

Model: They certainly do. But we will show they're bad.

Director: Is showing even a little bit of their bad much?

Model: It's like a thread you pull that unravels the weave.

Director: So we'll search out little bad things.

Model: And let them lead to greater things.

Director: And in the case of philosophy, we'll be looking for little bad beliefs.

Model: Right. And we'll question them. And if we're lucky, someone will eventually undermine the entire bad system of belief.

Director: But these things take time.

Model: Unless we're living in interesting times.

Director: Point taken. But aren't you afraid of what happens when an entire system of belief collapses?

Model: Look at the Soviet Union. That tells me what's at risk. I wouldn't like to live there now.

Director: Would you like to have lived there then?

Model: No. But it's worth noting I can live wherever I want. I choose to live in the United States. It has great problems, but it also has great people.

Director: Spoken like a patriot.

Model: You don't agree?

Director: I agree about the problems. But I would temper the great people part a bit. There are some great people here. Not all the people are great.

Model: Well, who can argue with that?

Director: Politicians often do. They like to brush the less-than-great aside and focus on the great—so much so that you wonder if a non-great person is to be found.

Model: So what do I say? 'I want most of you to vote for me, but I don't believe most of you are great.'

Director: If you could get elected on that, I would count you... great.

~ GREAT

Model: The people are used to being told they're great. Politicians—no, most people—are afraid not to tell the people they're great. Why do you think that is?

Director: Because the people rule.

Model: No they don't. The rich rule.

Director: Funny how we can disagree on something so basic concerning our country. Maybe there's a sort of marriage between the two?

Model: I'd love to see the pre-nuptial agreements there. But no, there's no marriage.

Director: How do the rich rule?

Model: People love money; the rich have it; and so the people look up to the rich and let them rule.

Director: The rich love power; the people have it; and so the rich look up to the people and let them rule.

Model: You can't be serious.

Director: Why not?

Model: I don't care who has what—the rich never look up to the people.

Director: That's where I think you're wrong. Haven't you heard the rich justify themselves in the terms of the people? Isn't that an act of subservience to power?

Model: What are you talking about? Trickle-down economics?

Director: As one example of many, sure. The wealth of the rich creates jobs and wealth for the people. Why justify their riches like this if they didn't have to?

Model: But they'd say it's not a justification. They'd say it's simply the truth.

Director: They protest a little too much for me to believe them in that. Are you a believer?

Model: No. So the people rule the great?

Director: The great rule the rich.

Model: But we were just saying most people aren't great.

Director: And it's true. But when they unite? They become a leviathan of sorts.

Model: And not to flatter one is to insult them all.

Director: That's about the size of it. There are, of course, important exceptions.

Model: Criminals and the mentally ill.

Director: Yes, but many people—millions and millions—are mentally ill these days.

Model: Sure, but I'm talking about those who are institutionalized.

Director: You mean those who go to public school?

Model: Ha, ha, You know what I mean.

Director: I do. Are there others besides criminals and the mentally ill?

Model: Those who lack honor.

Director: Ah. An important exception. Why aren't they great?

Model: They're not playing along.

Director: What does that mean?

Model: They don't unite.

Director: But why?

Model: I don't know exactly. There's just something about them that resists.

Director: Maybe it takes effort to unite?

Model: That might be it. You can't bond well with others unless you have self-control. Otherwise people are just all over the place and not *e pluribus unum*.

Director: They have to act as one?

Model: They have to think and act as one.

Director: Acting as one makes sense. But how do you think as one?

Model: You share common values?

Director: But is holding a value really thought?

Model: It means to have a certain way of looking at things.

Director: That's more the thing, I think. So what's the way?

~ Ways

Model: For one, you agree that all people have dignity.

Director: Except for those who don't.

Model: Right. And those who don't are those without honor.

Director: So it should really be something like this. All people can have dignity if they want.

Model: I think that rings true. But people would probably add a 'truly' in there.

Director: So it's, 'All people can have dignity if they truly want.' What does the 'truly' mean?

Model: It means you have to fight for your dignity.

Director: Fight for respect.

Model: Yes, there's really no difference here.

Director: Those who aren't willing to fight aren't part of *e pluribus unum*.

Model: Freedom isn't free.

Director: It's true. Freedom isn't free.

Model: We have to fight for freedom.

Director: Except those of us blessed with good looks?

Model: There's some truth in that.

Director: And except those of us who inherit great wealth?

Model: Truth again. But many of them spend their lives trying to prove they're worthy of their wealth.

Director: What's wrong with that?

Model: Why can't they just enjoy it privately and well? That's what I'd do. In fact, that's what I do with the wealth I have.

Director: Until I come along and fill your head with dangerous thoughts.

Model: They'd be dangerous if I had ambition.

Director: You really have no ambition?

Model: I don't.

Director: That makes you more of a catch. So why do it? Why run?

Model: I'm curious about what's possible.

Director: That's it?

Model: That and I want to fight for the cause.

Director: Ah, that's better. You know, about the ambition, I once had dinner with a nun—

Model: Excuse me. But how did you manage that?

Director: It's a long story. But during this dinner she and I differed concerning priests. I said they should have no ambition. She grew animated and said they certainly should.

Model: Did she say why?

Director: She said something about thus being better able to serve the Church. It makes me think about you.

Model: What do you mean?

Director: If word gets around that you really have no ambition, what will people think about how you'll serve the Nation? What if many think like the nun?

Model: Word will never get round.

Director: Why not?

Model: No one would believe it. All politicians have ambition.

Director: Why don't you?

~ AMBITION

Model: I don't know exactly. But I can't be the first politician to run without ambition. Why are you smiling?

Director: No reason. These politicians with ambition must have had strange circumstances.

Model: And mine aren't? My alliance with you?

Director: Why, Model, are you saying I'm strange?

Model: You're unusual for sure. Do you have ambition?

Director: Only for the cause.

Model: So you're selfless?

Director: I wouldn't say that.

Model: Why not?

Director: I'm afraid the ghost of Ayn Rand will haunt me one night. Have you read her?

Model: I have. I think at first she was very, very good. But then she got a little too preachy.

Director: Why do you think she became that way?

Model: She was the head of a movement. That's something I'll never be. Our cause isn't a movement, is it?

Director: In the sense that it fights inertia it is. But a political movement? No.

Model: So when people ask me what I'm fighting for, what shall I tell them?

Director: You already know the answer. Just start stating your positions on the issues. That's your fight, as far as the world is concerned.

Model: But as far as my friends are concerned?

Director: You're ambitious for the cause.

Model: I've often wondered what it's like to have ambition. People are driven by it, aren't they?

Director: Like demons.

Model: Demons. That's a good Dostoevsky book. Have you read it?

Director: Several times. The censored scene is the best.

Model: The one with Tikhon? I completely agree.

Director: In a way, that book is about ambition, perverted ambition.

Model: That and suicide.

Director: And you've contemplated suicide.

Model: Have you?

Director: Yes. What did you conclude?

Model: I'd rather stick around and see what happens. How about you?

Director: I can't serve the cause if I'm dead.

Model: That's really what you thought?

Director: Really, yes.

Model: So your ambition for the cause saved, or saves, your life?

Director: I'm not sure I'd call it ambition.

Model: Are your times often bleak?

Director: Only on occasion.

Model: Everything is on occasion. How often do you need to pull through? Once a month? Once an hour?

Director: It varies.

Model: Have you had suicidal thoughts while you've been here with me?

Director: No. I've been wholly absorbed in our talk.

Model: I hear writers are often like that. Everything is bleak except for when they write.

Director: I guess it depends what they're writing.

Model: And I guess for you it depends to whom you talk and what they say.

Director: Don't forget how they look.

Model: Ha, ha. I know you better than that.

~ SUICIDE, LUCK, THE CAUSE

Model: Good looking people often kill themselves.

Director: Why do you think that is?

Model: They can't live up to people's expectations.

Director: Is that the only reason?

Model: No, of course not.

Director: Do you feel the pressure from people's expectations?

Model: If I did, would you encourage me to run for office?

Director: Yes.

Model: Why?

Director: Better to have the expectations out in the open. Your imagination of what they are makes them worse.

Model: That's a good point. I don't think I would have thought of that on my own.

Director: We make a good team.

Model: We do. Promise me something?

Director: If I can.

Model: When things get bleak for you, you'll tell me?

Director: Alright. How will that help?

Model: We'll rack our brains and find new and better ways to serve the cause.

Director: Sometimes the cause seems hopeless.

Model: It wouldn't be a cause worth fighting for if it didn't. Does that sound glib?

Director: It sounds true.

Model: Good. We'll help each other through.

Director: When do things seem bleak to you?

Model: When it seems there's no point to life.

Director: How often does that happen?

Model: Every few days.

Director: What gets you out of it?

Model: I try to focus on simple pleasures.

Director: That works?

Model: Not really. I guess it just takes time for it to pass. But I'm hoping fighting for the cause will help.

Director: I think there's an excellent chance it will.

Model: Then I'm in luck.

Director: We're both in luck.

Model: We're going to need some luck on the campaign.

Director: Why?

Model: What do you mean, 'Why?'

Director: We'll be fighting a fight we know how to fight.

Model: Sure, but everyone can use a little luck.

Director: Yes, but you said we'll need luck as if we'll be in special need. I don't think we will.

Model: Why not?

Director: We're not afraid to lose. There will be no pressure on us here.

Model: What about our supporters?

Director: They'd like to see us win, but they won't be counting on us.

Model: Why not?

Director: Because they don't expect that politics is what will improve their lives.

Model: It's the cause that will?

Director: That's our message, aside from the issues.

Model: We'll talk openly about the cause?

Director: Maybe that's not wise. Instead, let's demonstrate what it is.

~ Demonstration, Alignment

Model: What if people don't understand what they're seeing?

Director: Then they don't belong to the cause.

Model: But even if they belong, is it something that will take time to learn?

Director: No and yes. No, those who belong will recognize it right away. Yes, they have to learn what it means to their lives.

Model: How long did it take you to learn after you first saw it demonstrated?

Director: I'm still learning.

Model: I see. We're always learning when we belong to the cause.

Director: Yes, it's true. At least *I* haven't stopped.

Model: This learning might drive away the bleakness.

Director: Yes, but sometimes it can be the source of bleakness.

Model: How?

Director: We might learn we were wrong about something important.

Model: But it's better to know than go on living in untruth.

Director: And that's why we keep on.

Model: What's the best way to demonstrate the cause to someone?

Director: You work with small, everyday things. You gently challenge something they say, something they're not likely to get upset about—something you know they've got wrong.

Model: How they take it says a lot.

Director: Yes. But if they take it well, or at least pretty well, you gradually work your way up to more significant things.

Model: What's the goal you're working toward?

Director: You want them to develop a taste for the work.

Model: So they can in turn perform it with others?

Director: Yes, but first they have to perform it on themselves.

Model: With the goal of getting rid of all bad belief. And you think our campaign can stimulate this.

Director: I do.

Model: Suicide is the result of a bad belief.

Director: What's the belief?

Model: That somehow life is bad.

Director: Maybe there's another belief.

Model: What?

Director: That hope doesn't exist.

Model: But the absence of hope is the absence of belief. Hope is a belief.

Director: We might also say hope is a feeling.

Model: If hope is a feeling it's not a belief.

Director: Maybe all beliefs are feelings at heart.

Model: All beliefs aren't really beliefs?

Director: Well, it's hard to say that.

Model: Maybe true beliefs are feelings and false beliefs aren't.

Director: You mean false beliefs don't align with a feeling?

Model: Alignment, yes. That's the thing.

Director: What happens when things align?

Model: Chemistry.

~ CHEMISTRY, CRISIS, SHOCK

Director: Good chemistry.

Model: Of course.

Director: Brain chemistry?

Model: Yes, though more than the brain is involved.

Director: Beliefs affect the body?

Model: And soul.

Director: I think there's truth in that. But now I'm not sure belief is a feeling.

Model: Why not?

Director: Because we can hold on to a belief through thick and thin, but feelings often change.

Model: Peripheral feelings, perhaps. But core feelings? Or the one core feeling of our lives?

Director: You have a point. Do you think a change in core belief can change that feeling?

Model: Yes, but maybe the feeling changes first and then the belief.

Director: Maybe the change in feeling creates what people call a crisis of faith.

Model: Yes, that's a good point. But either way—feeling first, belief first—we might have a crisis of faith.

Director: Yes, I suppose it doesn't matter which comes first. We'll probably never know. But tell me. How can we change someone's feelings?

Model: We expose them to a new point of view.

Director: That's it?

Model: This involves exposing them to new people, places, ideas—everything new.

Director: All at once?

Model: Sometimes a shock is needed to wake them up.

Director: Won't this disorient them?

Model: Sure, but isn't that better than being suicidal?

Director: Suicide? Is that our concern?

Model: Yes, but figuratively. People can kill themselves inside, you know.

Director: So we give them shock therapy. What do they need after that?

Model: Time, time to themselves to make sense of it all.

Director: How much time?

Model: Years, maybe a lifetime. But the point is that they'll want to live.

Director: We will have given them a long lasting gift.

Model: True, but they give us one in return.

Director: What?

Model: Proof that we're not crazy in our point of view.

Director: The cause.

Model: Yes. It's important that we get this validation. We're dealing with something that's somewhat obscure and hard to explain. Without validation we have to wonder.

Director: Wonder if we've lost touch with reality.

Model: Right.

Director: And we know we're in touch when our friends' chemistry starts to improve.

Model: Exactly so. We can check in on them from time to time. If their mood is becoming more stable and good, we have reason to think we know what we're doing.

Director: So we're doctors of sorts, treating the chemistry of bad belief.

Model: Yes.

~ MELTING

Director: Explain to me how the shock treatment works.

Model: First I have to say, the shock comes from good feelings.

Director: I thought the shock was supposed to wake them up, as happens when doused with cold water. Is that a good feeling?

Model: It is when what follows is good.

Director: So there's some unpleasantness followed by good, making the unpleasantness seem worthwhile.

Model: Exactly. And the good melts the ice around the heart.

Director: What's the effect of that?

Model: The person opens to friendly encounters with others.

Director: Hmm. And these friendly encounters alter their chemistry?

Model: Like nothing else can.

Director: Are you hoping to find friendly encounters through the campaign?

Model: I am. Are you?

Director: Definitely. But are we simply looking for encounters, or do we want something more?

Model: We want to develop loving friendships.

Director: Is there anything that might go wrong?

Model: The ones we encounter might be spooked by our dedication to the cause.

Director: They might run away.

Model: Yes.

Director: But if they run, maybe they'll still take the time to learn from the encounter.

Model: That's what we have to hope.

Director: Should we follow up with them?

Model: That might spook them even more.

Director: So what do we do? Just leave them alone?

Model: I think we have to. But some of them might come back.

Director: If they do, are they embarrassed that they ran?

Model: Maybe. But they have more hope than shame.

Director: Because now their heart is nice and warm. Well, Model, it seems we're going to have quite the campaign.

Model: We are.

Director: We're going have a traveling heart shock circus. The election is just an excuse.

Model: Do you mean it?

Director: I mean it.

Model: Well, I'm already on board.

Director: I think we're going to have a very good time.

Model: The time of our lives. And imagine if we win!

Director: It's possible, I think. We'll be a strong contributor to global warming.

Model: Heart warming, yes. And with all that ice melting, coastal cities will be at risk!

Director: Then we should start with those cities first, while they're still here.

Model: Where do you think we'll have the greatest success?

Director: Philosophy has a role to play wherever it finds itself.

Model: Yes, yes. Of course. But the real success is in the cities, and especially the universities in those cities. Right?

Director: That's where philosophy is most visible. But it can have great effect in even in very small towns.

Model: I don't see how. Everyone knows your business there.

Director: And so philosophy must be discreet.

~ Running Away

Model: I can't help but wonder if this is what happens with certain run-aways, of whatever age, from small towns.

Director: What do you mean?

Model: They have a sort of philosophical conversion and realize they must leave.

Director: Well, with some of them I'm sure that's possible.

Model: And now I think I have an answer to one of the questions I might be asked.

Director: What's the question?

Model: What is your favorite charity?

Director: What is it?

Model: A shelter for runaways.

Director: Which one?

Model: One that you and I will create.

Director: I see. Aside from the basics, what will this shelter provide?

Model: Sessions on philosophy, taught by you.

Director: No.

Model: What? Why not?

Director: I will not teach. Who am I to teach? But I will likely learn very much from those we shelter.

Model: Maybe you can moderate discussions? Direct the talk?

Director: That sounds much better. It might be something that keeps the ice from my heart.

Model: We'll be giving them a chance. We'll encourage them to get jobs, go to school, establish themselves in the world.

Director: If we win the election maybe some of them can come and work with us.

Model: Can you imagine how loyal they would be?

Director: I'm imaging how effective they would be. But as for loyalty? I'd rather most of them spread like seeds in the wind, some landing here, some landing there. The only loyalty I'd expect is in their memories of us.

Model: Why not have them near?

Director: We want philosophy to fan out throughout the land, not concentrate in one place.

Model: Because a little is much.

Director: A little might be all. But there's a problem.

Model: What problem?

Director: What if people run away with the express purpose of coming to our shelter?

Model: You mean if it weren't for us, they wouldn't have run away? That is a problem. How can we prevent it?

Director: Maybe we have two entities. The shelter, and a school.

Model: The school allows people to legitimately leave home and come to us.

Director: Yes, but now I'm having second thoughts.

Model: What's wrong?

Director: Schools and shelters are highly regulated. It's not just anything goes. This might not be as good an idea as we think.

Model: We can make it work. But I think we should combine the two.

Director: The runaways and the students?

Model: Yes. They can learn from each other.

Director: I hope so, because there's going to be a flood.

Model: A flood?

Director: Of people coming in.

Model: Why?

Director: 'Why,' asks the famous model and political candidate, 'why would anyone want anything to do with something connected with me?'

Model: I might capsize the ship. So I'll be a silent partner.

Director: Word will get round if you visit the school even once.

Model: Maybe I only come in at the end of the day, with a chosen group of students, who are asked not to tell anyone who they saw.

Director: Do you think that would work?

Model: It has to.

Director: Why?

Model: Because I really need something to warm my heart.

~ PLANS

Director: But listen to us with all our crazy plans.

Model: If only a tenth of what we've discussed comes to pass, that will be much.

Director: I agree. And it's fun to talk about these things.

Model: Is it possible to plan to have fun? Or does it just happen?

Director: People plan to have fun all the time.

Model: Do they succeed?

Director: Sometimes.

Model: What gets in the way?

Director: Lies.

Model: What lies?

Director: For instance? Someone lies about what he or she thinks is fun.

Model: So if I say it would be fun to go on a hike, because I really enjoy hikes; and you say sure, it would be fun, even though you don't like to hike; we'd be in for trouble, then?

Director: Right. My motives aren't pure.

Model: Fun aside, pure motives are important for any plan. Are your motives for the campaign pure?

Director: You should know by now that the cause is more important to me than the campaign. The campaign is a tool, an elaborate, expensive, exhausting tool—but a tool nonetheless.

Model: I know. I think we've been very honest with one another.

Director: I want to be more honest. If it weren't for your looks we wouldn't be having this conversation.

Model: This conversation about the campaign, or this conversation in general?

Director: Both.

Model: Director, you can't mean it. You're my friend only because of my looks?

Director: I do mean it. But I'm not your friend only because of your looks. Your looks are part of who you are, just as my looks are part of who I am. My point is that you can't hide from your looks. You have to accept your looks. We all have to accept our looks and move on.

Model: Well, you're preaching to the converted. I understand what you're talking about. And I can promise you I'm solid here.

Director: Good, because there can be no doubt. If there is, the campaign will bring it out and things will get bad.

Model: Bad for me or bad for the campaign?

Director: It's a healthy sign that you don't identify yourself with the campaign. The campaign is a separate thing from you or me or anyone else. This fact provides a good defense.

Model: How so?

Director: If they attack you they're really just attacking the campaign.

Model: That's true. I like thinking about it that way. And I'm sort of used to it already.

Director: How so?

Model: Modeling. If they attack what I'm wearing, they're not attacking me. Similarly, I'll be wearing the campaign. Attack it all they like, they won't get through to me.

Director: Excellent. So we can plan our campaign without your ego as a concern.

Model: Good. But we'll plan it to play to my strength?

Director: Yes, just as the clothing you model is tailored to you, so too the campaign.

\- TAILORING

Director: That's the trouble with teaching philosophy, you know.

Model: What trouble?

Director: A philosopher must tailor the talk to the audience.

Model: So you can obviously do a better job tailoring for one than a crowd.

Director: A crowd however small, yes.

Model: Then how can philosophers write?

Director: They always keep someone in mind.

Model: So one book might have one person in mind, and another book might have another?

Director: Yes. Or one chapter might have one person in mind, and another may have another.

Model: But the problem is that the book will resonate best only to those people.

Director: Unless there are others like them.

Model: But I know you well enough to know you like your friends to be unique.

Director: Here's how I look at it. Certain people, when confronted with the unique—a chapter, say—want to bring out their own uniqueness, too.

Model: So the writing provides encouragement.

Director: Yes, at best.

Model: At worst?

Director: The writing turns people off.

Model: Off to philosophy. Why would it do that?

Director: It's too difficult to follow.

Model: Because it uses big words and convoluted sentences?

Director: No, not so much that, though that can be a problem. I was thinking it's the array of concepts presented. If a concept is introduced in an unexpected place, it takes effort to make sense of that.

Model: So if this happens frequently, the book seems difficult.

Director: Yes. But there's more to it than that.

Model: What else is there?

Director: Lack of gratuitous imagery. Good philosophy has a Spartan style.

Model: It's up to the reader to imagine what the author means.

Director: Yes, and many people don't like to exercise their imagination. They like things described in detail for them.

Model: Why not introduce more imagery?

Director: I'll explain it like this. A book might describe you as blonde, deep blue eyed, six foot two, with a chiseled face and very lean body with broad shoulders and narrow hips. But that doesn't do justice to your beauty. Poems would have to be written about it. And even then, it's better for the reader to imagine you themselves.

Model: I'll say. Because that's not at all how I look! But what's the real reason?

Director: You're a funny one. The real reason is we want to scare some people off. Who reads a book with little imagery?

Model: Someone who seriously wants to know what the book says.

Director: And if the book is saying something deeply controversial?

Model: More reason to scare some people away.

~ WORDS, STRENGTH

Director: Now do you see why I don't write? Who wants to be a philosophical scarecrow?

Model: Is spoken philosophy easier than written philosophy?

Director: It's probably more effective. But it might be harder.

Model: Why harder?

Director: You don't have time to craft the perfect sentence. You have to think and speak on the fly.

Model: But you're just looking for something that will do the trick.

Director: Well, yes. And I might have only one attempt before I fail. But if my interlocutor will only give me the slightest benefit of the doubt, I might be able to help them with much.

Model: How often do you get the benefit of the doubt?

Director: Not very often. And sometimes people are generous in one area and miserly in another.

Model: Where are they generous?

Director: When it comes to things that flatter them.

Model: And miserly?

Director: When it cuts against their grain.

Model: I'd like you to cut against my grain, so I can see what you mean.

Director: I've been trying all this while. It seems you have no grain. You're not wood. You're flesh and blood.

Model: What's an example of cutting against someone else's grain?

Director: Oh, it could be anything, really.

Model: Confronting their bad beliefs?

Director: Certainly.

Model: What are beliefs composed of?

Director: Words.

Model: But aren't they also composed of feelings?

Director: Words and feelings go together, yes.

Model: What if the words are dead wood?

Director: Then the feelings will either die or overcome the dead wood.

Model: What happens when they overcome?

Director: Most often? A single seed falls and becomes a living tree, a mighty oak.

Model: I somehow find that beautiful.

Director: It's a contest of strength.

Model: What do you mean?

Director: There are forces that will seek to strangle the seed as it becomes a shoot.

Model: Bad words? And the shoot is a good feeling?

Director: The two can't exist together for long. One eventually wins.

Model: I think that's true.

Director: Life is a contest of strength.

Model: It's just that not everyone knows what strength is.

Director: What is strength?

Model: I think you know.

Director: It doesn't hurt for you to say.

Model: Strength is the roots of a tree enlarging a crack in a foundation.

Director: What else?

Model: Strength is patience and perseverance.

Director: And?

Model: Strength is little by little for much in the end.

Director: Anything else?

Model: Strength is taking difficult steps toward love.

Director: Surely there's something more.

Model: Strength is life, and life is strength.

Director: Well, I'm pleased to hear none of it depends on looks.

Model: Ha!

Director: But seriously, looks played right can help.

Model: Then coach me how to play.

Director: I will. I'll start by telling you not to be too nice.

Model: What's wrong with being nice?

Director: Nice is fine; too nice makes you a liar.

~ TIDES

Model: How so?

Director: Too-nice wishes not to let others down. It's especially a problem for the good looking.

Model: Say more.

Director: People attracted to you will often project things onto you.

Model: Good opinions. And if I politely tell them they're mistaken?

Director: They won't believe you.

Model: Why?

Director: Because most good looking people wouldn't give them the time
of day.

Model: They wouldn't because the others aren't good looking?

Director: Yes. But because you're nice to the ugly, the ugly think good
thoughts about you.

Model: But if not for my looks...

Director: ... they might not give you the time of day.

Model: So what do I do?

Director: Whatever you do, don't lie just so you don't let them down.

Model: What happens to the campaign if I let everyone down?

Director: The thing is to spend as little time with them as you can. And
when you can't, you must be scrupulous with your words.

Model: Scrupulous?

Director: Answer their questions honestly, precisely. So, for instance, if they ask you if you like to fish, what would you say?

Model: I've seen interesting television shows about fish and fishing. But I've never gone fishing and I really have no desire to, unless it were with someone I find really interesting, so we could spend time together, with fishing as the excuse.

Director: Very good. Now, why do you think they asked you if you like to fish?

Model: Because they wanted me to come fishing with them.

Director: Yes, that's likely. So how do you think they'll react to your reply?

Model: I think I will have hurt their feelings, unless I agree to fish with them.

Director: If you accept the invitation, what would you accept it out of?

Model: Shame?

Director: Or maybe fear of bad consequences. Or maybe both.

Model: And so the tide created by niceness sucks me in.

Director: Has it happened to you before?

Model: You can't be very good looking and very nice and not have this happen to you.

Director: Is that why many models drip with sarcasm?

Model: It's one of the reasons, I'm sure. It's a sort of defense.

Director: Do you need to defend yourself against fishing? What if you like it?

Model: I'm open to surprise. But I mostly like to be on my own. Don't you think that will be a problem in the campaign?

Director: We're not going to over-schedule you. One event a day.

Model: People will think I don't care enough to try.

Director: Some will. Some will admire your lack of rabid ambition. It all depends on your attitude.

Model: Funny. My mother told me attitude is everything in life.

Director: I don't know about that. But I know it can help you in this campaign.

- ATTITUDE

Model: What's the difference between good attitude and bad attitude?

Director: Good attitude helps; bad attitude hurts.

Model: Is it really that simple?

Director: It really is.

Model: Okay. But what is attitude itself?

Director: That, too, is simple. Attitude is the degree to which you are open or closed.

Model: I've never heard it described that way before.

Director: You never asked me.

Model: So good attitude is open?

Director: Not necessarily. You don't want to be open to bad things. So sometimes good attitude is open, and sometimes it's closed.

Model: And sometimes bad attitude is open, and sometimes it's closed.

Director: Right. Your mother was wise.

Model: So what should I be open to?

Director: Philosophy.

Model: And closed to?

Director: Bad ideas.

Model: But isn't that a contradiction?

Director: How so?

Model: Philosophy deals almost exclusively with bad ideas. How can it deal with them if it's closed?

Director: I'm probably going to regret this, but here I go. Suppose philosophy is a castle, and a bad idea rides up. Philosophy pulls up the drawbridge. But it treats with the bad idea from the ramparts, treats with it in honesty and scrupulousness.

Model: Why would you regret that?

Director: Because philosophy isn't a fortress.

Model: What is it?

Director: Well beyond all metaphor.

Model: So what is it?

Director: All we've talked about today.

Model: I sense you have a bad attitude about this.

Director: You might be right. How can I, a philosopher, deny you, who asks what philosophy is, an answer? I want to have a good attitude here. So I'll tell you this. Philosophy is the troop that rides up to the castle while the drawbridge is closed.

Model: Hold on. Philosophy is a troop?

Director: Oh, just go with it here. Philosophy rides up and blows its horn. 'Come out and dialogue, friend!'

Model: Dialogue?

Director: How do you think philosophy operates? Anyway, they see our force is small, so they're confident enough to lower the bridge and come out.

Model: Isn't philosophy afraid?

Director: Philosophy is terrified, yes. But philosophy is brave. So out comes the enemy.

Model: Hold on. How do you know it's an enemy?

Director: Because we don't yet know it's a friend.

Model: Is that the assumption? If you're not a friend you must be an enemy?

Director: Many people today assume if you're not an enemy you must be a friend.

Model: I don't know if that's true.

Director: Well, let's test it on the campaign and see. Anyway, so out comes the enemy, and they ask us what we want.

Model: What do we want?

Director: Entry into the castle.

Model: Why?

Director: Because we'd like to know what's within.

~ WITHIN

Model: I'd like to know what's within. Is my attitude good?

Director: It depends what you do with your 'like'.

Model: What if I don't *like* to know what's within? What if I *love* to know what's within?

Director: Your attitude just got better.

Model: Is love always better than like?

Director: Here's how it seems to me. Love is always stronger than like. Think of the campaign. Do you want people to like you or love you?

Model: I don't know. I mean, what counts is that they vote for me.

Director: I thought what counted was the cause.

Model: Should they like the cause or love the cause? But before you answer that, do you like the cause or love the cause?

Director: I love the cause. Or do I?

Model: What do you mean?

Director: The cause is like oxygen to me. I need it in order to live. Do we go around saying we love to breathe?

Model: Those of us who suffer anxiety would say we love to breathe freely.

Director: Do you suffer from anxiety?

Model: Terribly at times, though it has gotten better.

Director: To what do you attribute the improvement?

Model: Better knowledge of life.

Director: Oh, I thought you were going to say you positioned yourself better in life.

Model: What do you think knowledge of life allows you to do?

Director: Can anxiety lead to suicide?

Model: It can, when it gets bad.

Director: So knowledge of life is very important.

Model: Of course.

Director: And acting on your knowledge of life is very important.

Model: Nothing more important, in my opinion.

Director: How do we gain knowledge of life?

Model: By being open to life.

Director: By having a good attitude.

Model: Yes.

Director: And there are parts of life we should close ourselves to?

Model: There are.

Director: How do we know what these things are?

Model: We have to trust our gut. If we're traveling along our way, open to life and all it holds, and someone approaches us that makes us feel uneasy, we should close up. We can talk to them from the rampart, so to speak, hear what they have to say. Who knows? They might persuade us to open up.

Director: And we might be fooled.

Model: Yes, that's true. But that's an important lesson in life, a lesson we need to learn.

Director: What happens if we don't learn the lesson?

Model: Our sense of when to open up never develops.

Director: What's more common? To open too easily or to close too easily?

Model: Definitely to close too easily.

Director: Why do you think that is?

Model: Because most people are afraid.

- END

Director: What makes someone afraid?

Model: The other.

Director: I am not handsome; you are beautiful. We are other. Why are we not afraid?

Model: We have something more important in common.

Director: Philosophy?

Model: And all it entails.

Director: So we are not other. Other would be those who don't know philosophy. Are we afraid of them?

Model: I am. But I open myself enough to learn.

Director: But what if you've learned all you can learn? Do you keep on opening up?

Model: How would I know I've learned all I can learn?

Director: When you keep on seeing the same old thing over and over again. But have a look from the rampart. See if you see something new.

Model: Is that what you do?

Director: Yes.

Model: But I thought you said philosophy isn't a castle.

Director: It isn't. But my poor human self at times must be. No one can be open to everyone. It's simply not possible. You'll be overrun—even by friends.

Model: Even by friends?

Director: Too much of a good thing can kill you. Didn't you know?

Model: But then the thing is no longer good.

Director: Yes, good and bad are fluid to a certain degree.

Model: I've noticed.

Director: Even our talk today. Too much can be no good.

Model: Is it time to break it off?

Director: It takes courage to make a good end.

Model: Then let's make one.

Director: Alright. But let's make an end that looks forward.

Model: Will you contact your friends about me?

Director: I will, as soon as I can.

Model: And you're sure they'll have an interest?

Director: I'm as sure as sure can be. But if I'm wrong, would you be devastated?

Model: I won't lie. I'd be disappointed. After all, we had a stirring talk.

Director: We did, didn't we? But try to see that as worth it for its own sake.

Model: I know what you mean, and I will.

Director: So let's see what our friends say. And if they're not thinking of exactly the role for you we had in mind, I have no doubt there are other good roles to play. And let's not forget about philosophy.

Model: How could I forget? So if we don't get the candidacy, I expect us to stay in touch about dialogues we might have with others. I'd be willing to fly into town in order to have a good conversation, you know.

Director: Then it's lucky you have money so that you can afford such things.

Model: Truly. But, you know, I feel there's so much more we can say here right now.

Director: That makes for hope.

Model: Hope is infinitely better than having nothing left to say.

Director: Agreed. So farewell for now. And may our hopes, like dreams, come true.

Printed in the United States
by Baker & Taylor Publisher Services